The Chocolate Fast

*Embracing Your Bliss One
Truffle at a Time*

Stasia Bliss

BALBOA.
PRESS

A DIVISION OF HAY HOUSE

Balboa Press books may be ordered through booksellers or by contacting:

Balboa Press
A Division of Hay House
1663 Liberty Drive
Bloomington, IN 47403
www.balboapress.com
1-(877) 407-4847

ISBN: 978-1-4525-4033-7 (e)
ISBN: 978-1-4525-4034-4 (sc)
ISBN: 978-1-4525-4035-1 (hc)

Library of Congress Control Number: 2011918331

Printed in the United States of America

Balboa Press rev. date: 11/07/2011

Contents

PART 4
Navigating Your Divine Strata

PART 5
The Chocolate Fast: The Experience

PART 6
Superfluous and Delicious

This book is dedicated to my beautiful son Heritage, who is every day a reminder of what it means to live life from a place of true Bliss. Thank you my dear for joining me on this ecstatic journey!

~Chocolate~

Increases sensuality and beauty
Helps to heal and open the heart
Nourishes the intellect and attracts prosperity

Caution - - Disclaimer - - Personal Health Observation - -

There are certain persons who should NEVER fast without professional supervision. For example:

Persons who are physically too thin or emaciated.

Persons who are prone to anorexia, bulimia, or other behavioral disorders.

Those who suffer weakness or anemia.

Persons who have tumors, bleeding ulcers, cancer, blood diseases, or who have heart disease.

Those who suffer chronic problems with kidneys, liver, lungs, heart, or other important organs.

Individuals who take insulin for diabetes, or suffer any other blood sugar problem such as hyperglycemia.

Women who are pregnant or nursing.

The information in this book is not intended to diagnose, cure or heal you. Please see your medical professional, for they have the legal right to say they can do these things. Or you can take responsibility for your own health.

Preface

What you are about to read has been a playful, joyful work for me, as well as a life-changing journey. In the creation of it, I have compiled many little gems of wisdom accumulated over the years in my pursuit of transformation and 'enlightenment'. This book is a reflection of my quest for connectivity and at-ONE-ment – which are really the same thing - and in many respects, you are meeting me through the words on these pages. Hello!

The experience of writing a book for the first time has been amazingly challenging. I have the deepest gratitude and respect for my editor and partner for much of this journey, David Brown IV for assisting me in arranging my stream of thoughts into a more "intellectually palatable form, filtering out the larger excesses and offenses to the English language." (He made me write that verbatim.) Sometimes our moments of purest self-expression can be a little too raw for consumption by the general public. This is one of the few instances where some "cooking" of original materials is definitely called for.

I want to thank you, the reader, for supporting me by following me down this remarkable path that I've been Blissed to find. It is my sincere desire that you feel filled up through the reading of this book—and ultimately, by doing a chocolate fast yourself. For I feel there is nothing I could say with mere words that would be able to compare with your own transcendent experience.

If you are reading this book, I am guessing you love chocolate as much as I do. Let's see if we can't get over what we think is "right" in this situation and just embrace the fact that we truly love something. When we love something, and we deny ourselves that thing, we are in truth denying a part of ourselves.

Besides, haven't you heard?...Chocolate is good for you!

So, let's eat chocolate together for a whole day without guilt, shame or remorse and see what happens...let's eat chocolate for a whole day with an attitude of gratitude, appreciation and celebration. Forget, just for a day, all the 'bad' things you have believed, heard, read, and felt about chocolate and eating it. Imagine instead that you are on a deserted island with nothing to eat, and you have just discovered the amazing food known as chocolate. Eat it like it is the jewel and treasure it is. Enjoy it fully, without holding back and without thought of possible negative effects. Eat it like it is your last day eating EVER! You will feel liberated!

Take a moment right now with me and imagine yourself in front of a chocolate counter with every possible selection of chocolaty delights available to you. Allow yourself to forget any reason why you have chosen to not eat chocolate in the past. Just let that all go right now...See the chocolate, which has been prepared in every conceivable way, and it is there for you to choose, at no cost. Scan the glass display case: see the layer cakes, truffles, brownies, ganaches and tortes. How about some chocolate cream pie, triple fudge or soufflé? Let the smell of chocolate waft into your open nostrils and feel the chemicals in your body already beginning to change; feel the smile creeping over your face without prompting, sense the excitement in your belly. Allow yourself in this moment to be as a child, free of the confines and limitations of the mind, of the all-too-adult concept of 'appropriate' behavior. Imagine yourself ordering up the desserts of your choice and taking them into an adjoining room. This room, that you now enter, is also fixed up just as you would like. The decorations, furnishings, music—everything is to your particular taste. When you enter this room it is as if the outer rooms have disappeared and you are here alone with your chocolate. Imagine spotting the most delightful place to sit, with the perfect arrangement of eye-pleasing platters on which to place your desserts, your ambrosia of fragrant splendor. Sitting yourself down in front of the chocolate, move your awareness closer and closer and inhale the aroma, lose yourself in the details of the artistry in this creation. Allow yourself to notice the music which accompanies you and adds to the perfection of this moment: your perfect soundscape for this adventure.

In your mind, imagine now feeling open and grateful for this moment, created just for you and your enjoyment. Feel yourself present with the beauty and the magic. Picking up your chosen morsel, move the blessed gift into your mouth and feel how it melts, moistens, and moves in your mouth. Notice the textures and sweetness. As you revel in the sensations, feel as though you are being transported into another time and place…a timeless space of *Bliss* and abiding wholeness. Notice the sensitivity of your skin and your hearing…feel all your senses heightened. And as you swallow, give a silent or audible sigh of awe, confirming your joy and pleasure in life in this moment.

Can you imagine a whole day like this?

Why do we deny ourselves such pleasure? Is it Programming? Social constructs? Dietary regulations? Belief in limitations? As children we innocently incorporated the ideas of those who appeared wiser due to time spent here on this planet before us. We are not children anymore.

If we looked around at the studies today, if we dug down deep in our past, if we listened both far and near to the words spoken of this subject here... we would learn of the magic, we would be taught of the *Bliss*, we would hear tales of its majesty, we would hear stories of a kiss. It is not for nothing that chocolate has been given a most cherished place in all of time and in our hearts. Though guilt threatens to take that away, the blessings of chocolate still surpass the shame.

Come take a journey with me, if you dare, to learn of the things to demystify fear of the chocolate so sweet and so glorious to taste. Dear Chocolate, it's time to take your rightful place!

Powerful power
Hourless hours upon hours
Of this
Bliss.
Suddenly
Gently
Swimming within me
Directing me-
'Just Be'.
Flowers all around and all over
Giant explosion
Of what to discover
Awakening...
To nothing routine
Only sensitizing
Realizing
Clearing-out-the-clutter
Learning not to stutter
At life.
Clarifying
Darifying
Never any question
Unless I stay behind – in my mind.
Well up inside
Passionate
Ecstaticate
Hyper-sensiate
Let the center
be the soothing lotion
to this spiritual commotion
ride the spine
internal highway of mine
Straight line.
...
Waves can find the shores
Of my skin

Waves of all this energy
I spin in
Electrifying
Evolvifying
Spirit rising.
We are the magic
We thought we didn't believe in.
It's making it's way
To our fingers
Our lips
Becoming our words
And the distance we aim for.
Kiss the breeze
Hear the cells dance in your toes
Smell it in your nose.
Consciousness is
Everything I am
And you are
And
Finally
Softly
Majestically
Inwardly and outwardly
Spiraling
And Climbing
I AM
Becoming
We are opening
The Eye
..
Rooted
We Fly.

~Stasia

At the beginning of each chapter you will find a short meditation. These meditations are meant to connect you on a deeper level to the information presented here. Enjoy!

26. Wheel of Self-Respect

Angel Sigil

HU-MISH-BELVEK

Part 1

Layers of Chocolate

Before moving into this chapter, take a few deep breaths. Feel yourself relaxing more into your chair or standing position. Bring your attention to the bottoms of your feet. If they are not touching the ground already, go ahead and reach your feet out and place them on the floor. Imagine opening up the bottom of your feet to receive an invisible flow of energy, as if from the Earth, into your body via your feet. Take a moment to connect to the Earth in this way. Breathe. Connecting to our feet offers us a simple way to feel 'grounded' and supported. In a very real way, we are being supported, held up by this planet every moment. Continue to breathe in this support, expressing gratitude with every exhalation.

Chapter 1

Opening

In the pure and holy embrace of Anything, we find our truest Self.

What if we could fully embrace the joy that comes with eating chocolate, without any sense of guilt, for an entire day? Could we then also embrace other experiences of joy? This is where we begin, with this thought, this question:

What if?

For many of us, our relationship with chocolate is not unlike our relationship with ourselves—with our most natural and authentic self, that is. How willing are we to surrender to the state of divine Bliss that is at the very core of our innermost being? Do we not, for the most part, limit ourselves with regard to the experience of pleasure and ecstasy? How often do you allow yourself the experience of joy—pure joy? Would you go so far as to say that you allow yourself to experience Bliss? I know, that's a tough one—a BIG one. What is it about that word, Bliss?

The surname I bear now is not the one I was born with. When I first began to think about changing my last name to Bliss, it was a very exciting prospect. In my core I felt certain it was going to require a shift in my consciousness, a change in perspective to feel comfortable and 'deserving of' calling myself Bliss. To say every day to everyone I meet: 'I am Stasia Bliss', that would take some getting used to. Yet as I began to be open to the prospect of accepting my Bliss, and I began to embrace myself as 'Bliss,' I also began to move into a space, not just of acceptance, but of the realization that Bliss is my divine birthright. It's yours as well.

A movement is taking place today that urges us to reach within and touch this place of inner peace and divine Bliss. Yoga, meditation, Tai chi, and a host of other like spiritual practices both ancient and new are now (finally!) starting to come to the forefront of our modern reality here in the West. And all of them teach in one form or another that Bliss is our birthright, our natural state of being.

Isn't there just something about the idea of Bliss, of the very word Bliss, that resonates deep within? Beyond all the self-judgment and fear, something that says 'Yes, I deserve to live in state of Bliss!' ?

Well, that's because YOU DO!

If you are at the beginning of this road to inner discovery, let me suggest an experiment. Take an already recognized pleasure in your life—journaling, gardening, origami, dancing, cooking, whatever it may be—and allow it more fully and completely into your life, without guilt and without shame. With such an acceptance of something that you already love, we can begin to build our association with the idea of Bliss. It is easier to go somewhere, mentally and emotionally, if you have some kind of reference point. For the journey of this book we are to use chocolate as the reference point for pleasure, joy and Bliss (though you may use anything you truly love in the same manner that we use chocolate here, as the *fast* is simply a 'concept' which can easily apply to any joy).

Throughout this journey I will continue to quote from a chocolate expert named 'Chloe' from the book <u>Chocolate: A Bittersweet Saga of Dark and Light</u> , for I resonate with her and find her statements charming. I hope you agree! She says:

> *Chocolate is extremely pleasurable…You have just to give yourself permission to enjoy it. As the bouquet of melting chocolate perfumes your palate, it spreads a feeling of well-being. Each of your five senses is excited, and they all interact with each other.*

Through chocolate you can get a glimpse of your natural state of Bliss. You already know this has happened, if you think about it, nearly every time you have eaten it. Think about it now, the chocolate melting in your mouth and coating your throat, the taste on your tongue. You feel the excitement, the satisfaction, the joy just in the thought of it. We might laugh a bit to ourselves, thinking we are being silly to believe real joy could be found through a dessert… And so, just as quickly as we feel the joy, we banish it and move into the feeling of guilt or remorse. Do we think we must balance our pleasure with something 'practical?' Is guilt practical? Do we feel so undeserving of pleasure that we are compelled to replace that feeling with one more 'fitting?'

Fitting?

Do we really believe that we deserve to feel guilt and pain, sickness and loss, rather than joy, pleasure and Bliss?!

Guilt, shame, worry, fear, and other forms of self-censure are all toxic emotions. Any distressing emotion causes our body to produce cortisol, a hormone that -when produced in excess (or kept in the body over an extended period of time) suppresses the immune system by shrinking the production of T-cells by the thymus gland.

Chocolate, on the other hand, is beginning to be recognized as one of the healthiest foods on the planet. In its raw form it is, in its physiological effects, both nutritive and tonic, and is now recognized to be a "superfood". (See David Wolfe's book <u>Naked Chocolate</u> & properties of 'superfoods').*

When we embrace that which brings us joy, it is not so much the thing that we are embracing that opens us up to Bliss, but the act of embracing itself. It is through this embracing that we allow an inner alignment to take place, bringing about the possibility of living from a higher expression of our Selves— from our true Bliss.

As you move forward into this book, keep your mind open to the possibility that chocolate can, indeed, be a doorway to your highest self. By the time you reach the end of the book, you may just decide to release the need for guilt in every area of your life, and embrace the Bliss that is your inheritance!

In the process of the personal transformation that has unfolded as a result of writing this book, these words have come to me:

And so it is, that in the pure and holy embrace of Anything, we find our truest Self.

27. Wheel of Self-Directed Desire of the Heart

<u>Angel Sigil</u>

INOMANA

Once again, take a few deep breaths. Take your attention now to your physical body, and especially to your hands. Become aware of your hands. Feel the way they are touching this book. Let your consciousness move into each digit: right thumb, left thumb, right index finger, left index finger, right middle finger, left middle finger, right ring finger, left ring finger, right pinky, left pinky.

Now bring attention once again to your hands in their entirety. Find a way to bring more relaxation into them while holding this book. Take a few deep breaths, maintaining your awareness in your hands. Now let's begin…

Chapter Two

Bliss?

So what is this "Bliss?" Our experience of Divine Being-ness or 'God' is intimately bound up with the feeling of Bliss, which could be described as partaking of the Divine. When we begin to let our bodies resonate with the word 'Bliss', initially we may find ourselves mentally categorizing it as an experience that is intangible, an incomprehensible idea or an idealistic destination. For some it is a familiar and readily attainable state. What makes this so? I would like to suggest that we are not only capable of bliss, but of Bliss. Can you feel the difference?

So…Bliss—What is it? What comes to mind when you think of 'Bliss?' What do you feel? To some, the word conjures up an image of the climactic experience: the rush, the high, the ecstasy that later leaves one feeling a more defined 'low,' like the effects of certain mind-altering drugs, or the sexual experience (for many), or perhaps a brush with death. This type of peak experience associated with an adrenaline rush is NOT what I am referring to when I speak of Bliss and our natural state. It would be exhausting to maintain that kind of heart-racing, adrenaline-pumping experience all the time.

In my life journey I have discovered within myself what I call 'deep yogic roots.' It has been a challenging and delightful process of self-study, and one which leads me to believe that I was a yogi in a past life (or several lives). For those of you who struggle with the idea of reincarnation, I would explain it as having a certain growing ease in drawing from the collective experience of centuries of yogic awareness: it is very familiar to me on a soul level, and feels perfectly natural to live 'yogically.'

In my personal experiences and studies I have come to understand Bliss as a state of deep and abiding peace, a *peace that expands*. This Bliss is such a pure and natural state that when immersed in it, even those things that would previously have elicited anger or pain are recognized for their ultimate blessing. All things become, in this state, impersonal or 'unattached' to an individual personality and 're-attached to' or remembered as part of a cosmic whole. The ups and downs start to equalize, not in a mundane way, but rather at a higher frequency of abiding union with all of life. For in this state of Bliss, one remembers that we are all connected on a deeper level. We are not separate from the creative force from which we sprung, we have merely forgotten our divine birthright and have accepted misery, stress and poverty as normal circumstances of this bodily existence.

Some argue that there could be no Bliss without this misery and sorrow; that opposition allows for both extremes. Emotional duality is very human, but we are more than merely humans: we are spiritual beings, capable of accessing states of awareness vibrationally higher than those we have known in the past.

When we experience emotional highs and lows we trigger a natural revulsion for those things we don't want to repeat (or create), and a desire for what we wish to create. In our desires we create mental images, which become our goals. The more we allow the Bliss experience back in, the more familiar we become with it. And like anything we repeat again and again, we start to create cellular memory for it, and it becomes 'the norm.' For example, if you have ever taken a yoga class you are likely familiar with the tightness your muscles felt when you first tried to get into those poses. After some time—days, weeks, months—you began to feel some opening and eventually, after doing the same stretch a hundred times, you found that you could practically 'fall' into it with ease, sometimes even out of class while in conversation with friends, or in your living room.

If you aren't a yoga person, perhaps you can relate more to the example of making your favorite recipe. After you have made it enough times, you don't even have to think about it or even measure the ingredients—you have created a form of 'cellular memory' for that recipe. How about riding a bike, learning a piece of music or driving your car to the same place every day? Cellular memory. Steven Thayer, founder of Integrated Energy Therapy, says of cellular memory:

> *"Every cell in our body has the ability…to remember. Our cellular memory can store the memory of physical traumas like accidents, cuts, bruises, surgeries or abuse; emotional trauma like heartache, fear, guilt and anger; and mental trauma that manifests in low self-esteem, unworthiness, worry, etc. When trauma is suppressed into the cellular memory, that energy can get stuck. The problem with suppressed cellular memory is not only does it limit our ability to live freely and joyfully in life but it can also support the body in developing physical illness."*

This gives us the understanding of cellular memory, but when looked at from a more positive, beneficial approach we can see that we can acquire this same kind of affinity or memory for experiencing Bliss.

At first we fully experience the ups and the downs—in all their often melodramatic glory—that we associate with being 'human.' This has been the 'blessing' of duality. But as we travel on this road toward discovering or 'remembering' Bliss, something starts to happen. We begin to have an opportunity to see things from a different perspective. We stop seeing everything in its small or 'reduced' egoic version—*my* house, *my* job, *my* relationship, *my* aches and pains. With the perspective of Bliss, we are endowed with the ability to experience the 'bigger picture'—the human family, our planet, our process, the whole. We begin to perceive the greatness expressing itself through the forms of all creation, and the 'impersonal,' loving, all-encompassing creative force behind and within it all.

Bliss begins to become the 'norm' when we stop striving to be something that we think we are not but should be, and start living from a place of joy. When I say stop striving, I don't mean to let go of motivation and action, but rather to start embracing who we are now. Instead of looking for the next best thing, the next 'look,' the next something that will give us that all-important edge: the faster, stronger, whiter and brighter, 'greener,' sexier, more technologically superior, better tasting, more nutritious— whatever. We can enjoy the pleasures of this world without depending on it for our fulfillment and source of happiness. Instead, we have the opportunity to embrace where we are now— to find the Bliss that is ours within this moment, and from this place of Bliss - truly appreciate all that is around us fully, in more depth than ever before!

In some religions the emphasis on what 'not' to do is so constraining and overwhelming that it often takes away from the possibility to live from the heart and in the moment. Self-judgment and criticism, fear and guilt find their way into the top four habitual emotions, crowding out the peace, happiness, empowerment and Bliss that are naturally ours. As we allow ourselves to experience more and more of the 'Big Picture' perspective, the harshness of duality doesn't disappear, but rather fades, eventually taking the form of contrasts on life's canvas. For example, when a great loss occurs (death, financial loss, divorce, etc.), even within the state of Bliss we still experience the emotions that need to be felt in all of their humanness. But now, human 'attachment,' as the Buddha calls it, does not triumph; and feelings of depression, abandonment and defeat do not conquer. Rather, the 'big picture' enters in and soothes the soul, bringing the knowledge of the opportunity for growth, heart opening and deeper understanding. For there is always another perspective from which to gain insight, especially on a perceived tragedy. What great comfort there is in the knowledge that we are more than this body, these thoughts and these emotions—we are infinitely Blissful beings, all connected, all part of a picture much greater than the drama of human reality that we are immersed in daily. And so, though we live within the dramas and emotional polarity of the human experience, we are not of it. It seems necessary to feel fully the separation of being human at times, for without these humbling moments in life we might not be compelled to remember the Union underlying everything.

Bliss is the ability to live peacefully with what is and see its greater meaning. Chocolate is just one of the many keys we can use to assist us in unlocking the door to our Bliss. It's all in the perspective.

So, let's get to the chocolate!

* * * * *

The primary mythology surrounding the origin of chocolate is simply delightful! See if you can relate to any of the perspectives in the fable below; let it give you some insight into your own beliefs about both chocolate and Bliss. This is the condensed version of the story I found in a children's book of Mayan folktales by Linda Lowery called *The Chocolate Tree*, and it is probably the best rendition of the origin of chocolate I have ever read. So, whether you are someone who celebrates the wisdom of folktales, or someone who just enjoys a good story, this ancient tale of chocolate is sure to give you a smile. And if you're like me, you won't mind a little additional 'historical' proof to validate your personal argument for chocolate as a divine substance.

THE GIFT OF CHOCOLATE

To the Maya of old, all crops came from the gods: corn, beans, squash, sweet potatoes, you name it. One of the great kings of Heaven would visit the people and bring them seeds from his home in Paradise. This great one was called Kukulkan, 'the feathered serpent.' He wore a cloak of colorful feathers and his skin was like that of a snake. Now, Paradise was where all the other gods and goddesses resided, but Kukulkan liked to spend his time with the Earth people, as he loved them so and wanted them to have their own paradise on Earth. (Isn't that nice?) He was the one, they say, who taught them to grow their crops and to enjoy the earth's bounty; who taught them of the calendar, and how to track the seasons. He also brought them music and dance.

The people loved and adored Kukulkan and built him a great temple. From the top of the temple the great king could leap through the morning star to visit Paradise and also return to Earth again. His people were so happy and gave him such honor that he wanted to give them something more.

In Paradise, the favorite nourishment of the gods and goddesses was chocolate (xocoatl), and it was prized above all other foodstuffs. Kukulkan wanted to bring this food to the people of the Earth, but many of the deities frowned on this, fearful that Earth would then be just like Paradise. Kukulkan thought this would be a positive thing, not something to be feared, so against the wishes of his divine family, he took one of the cacao trees from Paradise and brought it through the morning star to Earth.

He taught the Mayan people how to harvest the cacao seed and to work with the bean, grinding it and turning it to drinking cocoa. The Maya rejoiced at their new gift, and cacao was honored as the sacred beverage that it was among the gods. For the crime of sharing this divine substance with mere mortals Kukulkan was banned from returning to Paradise, and so he stayed with the Maya to help cultivate and distribute this piece of Paradise to the entire world.

Over time, the story continues, cacao came to be used as a form of currency, and the largest portion of this magnificent delight was reserved for the royalty's enjoyment. Recently, discoveries of ancient royal burial sites have found pots lined with residue of cacao, lending some credence to this story of chocolate's divine status. Moreover, its botanical name reflects this ancient tale, as chocolate came to be called *Theobroma cacao*: 'Food of the gods.'

What are the perspectives given here? Well…there is that of the Kukulkan—the Feathered Serpent God who brought chocolate to the Maya. Then we have the Mayan people who received the gift, praised its giver and enjoyed the substance as a holy elixir. Lastly, the other gods and goddesses of Paradise who wanted to keep the secret of chocolate to themselves out of fear that sharing it with those of Earth would somehow devalue their prized possession. The story is interesting in that there is only one representation of what would be considered a 'negative' or distressing emotion— and that is fear. The gods and goddesses feared losing their status through sharing. This fear is still associated with chocolate, showing up in the forms of guilt and shame, which are just other names for fear. These fears today are also associated with having done something to reduce one's status, only now it's in terms of health, self-control, beauty, etc. For example, believing that eating chocolate will make your skin break out, give you fat thighs or cause you to be sick are all common fears. As a society, we place value on beauty, self-control and health; therefore, eating chocolate to excess (more than a 'respectable' amount) would on some level mean a drop in 'status,' would it not?

The Mayan peoples, as they are portrayed here, represent a pure heart, total faith and gratitude. This is the attitude with which I would encourage each one of us to accept the gift of life, the gift of Self, even the gift of chocolate. Allow another aspect of yourself—perhaps your higher Self—to be like Kukulkan, bringing valuable cherished wisdom from other realms of understanding to be shared for your benefit, received with an open heart. Kukulkan shows up for each one of us whenever something resonates on a deeper level. It could be a book, an activity, a conversation, a moment. You know when these moments occur.

In my life, the path of surrender to that which brings me joy and Bliss is like the paradisiacal elixir. Raising my boy, being in the garden, sitting in meditation, relaxing with a cup of tea, writing this book, making chocolate, I am doing what I love, surrendering to it, and thereby aligning myself, opening myself up to receive the gift of Bliss.

The key to Bliss is in the receiving.

Take a moment to bring awareness now into your arms, your right arm and your left. Feel the energy that moves up and down your arms from your hands. Imagine opening your arms wide, and if you feel so inclined, take one hand out to the side to stretch it, and then the other…maybe both. Feel your capacity to embrace in this moment, with your arms. Follow that awareness down the chest now and breathe into your lungs – expanding the rib cage.

Chapter 3

Embracing

If Bliss is our natural state, then why does it seem that we are so averse to feeling it? The world sometimes seems like a game we are playing…and losing. Everything that makes us happy, expands our sense of Self and allows us to know our Bliss, we avoid. Everything that makes us sad and angry and hurt and feel fear, these things we seem perpetually to create. We must be doing it unconsciously, right? Surely we wouldn't act this way knowingly! It would appear that the only logical explanation for our behavior is that it is a learned behavior, the result of conditioning. If we were really conscious of our decision to avoid Bliss, we would correct it, would we not?

Chocolate.

Say it again to yourself…Chocolate.

Now aloud: 'Chocolate.'

Let the images come, the memory of its taste…the way it feels, melting on your tongue… Perfect. Without even eating a piece, we can, through memory or visualization, enjoy the Blissful experience of this sacred delight. No guilt, right?

Now think of the last time you ate some chocolate. Did you feel you had to sneak it? Did you eat too much and regret it afterward? Did you hog down the lot of the precious morsels? And how did you feel after your escapade? Were you able to enjoy the chocolate fully? I certainly hope so! However, it is the unfortunate truth that for many of us the experience of eating chocolate is often tied to the emotions of guilt and shame. In the last chapter, we briefly touched on the findings that distressing emotions such as guilt and shame are immune-suppressors. When we have these emotions we are perpetually telling the body that there is 'trouble', and our body keeps producing cortisol. You see, cortisol is a hormone produced during 'fight or flight' as a protection for the body. It boosts the immune system initially as well as increasing adrenaline, etc. After the 'attack' or episode is over, the body would naturally reduce the quantity of cortisol in the blood. By continuing to feel distressing emotions cortisol begins to have the reverse effect, we actually reduce the amount of white blood cells we produce, most importantly T-cells that guard against disease and infection.

We usually want to have dessert, and we may enjoy it while engaged in it, but somewhere in the back of our minds is that little voice counting calories, fearing later stomachaches and bloating and keeping us from taking the last bite. Somewhere in our programming we were taught to believe that we shouldn't eat 'too much' chocolate. Someone has convinced us that it is 'bad' somehow, only allowed in the smallest and most infrequent of doses. We describe the eating of it as an 'indulgence.' What does that even mean?

In our relationship with chocolate, our attitude is similar to the attitude we have toward hobbies or pastimes that we wish we had time for, but with which we limit our experience by arguing we have 'more important' things to do and 'greater responsibilities' to attend to. Yet the experiences we have while in the moment with these things which bring us joy are communications from our inner-most being: that we are in alignment, that we are living our purpose.

The term 'indulgence' derives from Roman Catholic theology, and is defined as "the full or partial remission of temporal punishment due for sins which have already been forgiven." An 'indulgence' was granted when the sinner had confessed and had received absolution. We still use our indulgences in the same way today. For example, with chocolate, if we have eaten well and managed to avoid having dessert all week, then we think we deserve to 'indulge' a little, right? We even refer to eating chocolate as being a little 'naughty.' We've all used the classic line (or something like it), "I've been good, so I deserve this slice of chocolate cream pie!"

No matter who we are or what our 'status,' we all have something in life we consider an indulgence. For some the indulgence is buying a favorite soap, or a fine bottle of wine. Our jobs or income may dictate our indulgences. For example, if you work at a bookstore, you might 'indulge' by spending your paycheck on books. Someone who works in retail clothing might do the same with clothing; a jeweler, with that diamond necklace she's been eyeing. The indulgence might take the form of property, if you work in real estate or an extra cup of coffee if you are barely making ends meet. Some might indulge by spending 'a lot of money'—more than one's income, a chunk of one's savings—but no matter what the level of income or supposed status, when it comes to dessert, and especially to chocolate, indulgence reaches across the board.

In Western culture, in this day and age, we have assigned chocolate—and desserts in general—a role in our lives that, I believe, derives from our childhood conditioning. Growing up, we were told we couldn't have it, that it wasn't good for us; that we would spoil our dinner, or that we would get sick if we ate too much. Abstaining from chocolate—taking a restrained approach to 'dessert'—was determined to be 'good' behavior. Eating chocolate was cast in a very negative light and became a 'sin,' really. As we matured, we began simply to consider chocolate one of the 'lesser evils,' but we never fully removed it from the 'list.' As adults, no one is telling us that we can't have it anymore, yet the guilt remains, and the inner struggle continues. We 'indulge' in chocolate now and feel ashamed for it afterward. Why? The excitement builds in anticipation of our 'due reward,' and then the shame crashes down on us for having eaten 'the whole thing.'

It is apparent to me that the issue isn't the chocolate. Clearly, it's bigger than that. It may be that chocolate represents a part of our 'whole' nature, a part we have consciously or unconsciously repressed. In this information age, surely we have all had the opportunity to realize that nearly all of us have repressed something. We may differ in apparent magnitude of our repressed 'whatevers,' but truth be told, we all have some aspect of ourselves that we have not allowed the light of awareness to shine upon.

Carl Jung and others speak of our 'shadow self'. There are many interpretations of what that is. My interpretation goes something like this: Think of what you would be like in your most Blissful state. How would you spend each day, what would you be doing, how you would appear? What are the feelings you would have? How would your breath be in this moment? Now juxtapose this picture of Bliss with where you are right now. I call this realization and the awareness produced by this juxtaposition, knowledge of the shadow self. In this knowing of what Bliss might look like for you, and the feeling of separation from it, you begin to recognize how you are living the mere shadow of your dream, in the shadow of your truth. In this knowing we become conscious of our shadow self. Our truest Self (or the illuminated Bliss self) many of us only glimpse on rare occasions, when something really excites us, or at moments when we feel the beginning of pleasure—but then some part of the situation or circumstance dictates to us that we should not feel that way. Unconsciously, we 'repress' the bubbling pleasurable emotions that threaten to place us at odds with what is 'acceptable.' Our true Self is where Bliss hides, under the layers of 'supposed-to's and 'shoulds.'

Did you ever find yourself sneaking dessert as a child? Who doesn't remember at least once hiding in a closet, or the bathroom, behind a door or chair inhaling the last brownie, chocolate chip cookie or spoonful of frosting? How many of us have had to hide our affection for another person? Or had to hide an entire relationship? Favorite clothing, a purchase we made? Some of us have felt that we had to hide serious decisions that brought us joy, feeling as though they would disappoint shame or hurt another. Our lives are full of these stories.

This hidden part of Self, when brought into the light of awareness, transforms us completely; for in order to have this awareness at all, we must be ready to fully embrace it's truth, the willingness to accept Bliss into our life.

As a child, when we were told something was 'bad,' many of us (if not all of us) on some level were curious. Taboos, despite their warnings, often entice. It is a natural response if one is curious and 'brave'—or rebellious—enough, when the opportunity arises, to try to find out for ourselves what is so 'bad' about something. Perhaps we transgress in order to really experience the 'bad.' Or maybe we do it in hopes of disproving this label through our own experience. If our experience shows us that our parents were 'right,' then they succeed in passing on their 'stuck story' (see below). However, if we experienced it differently, we usually did so in secret, keeping our 'indulgence' to ourselves.

The 'stuck story' concept has been passed down from Native American storytellers to illustrate how people keep perpetuating their miserably ineffective and disempowered status quo, repeating the same pattern of behavior and arriving at the same outcome again and again . According to the tradition, a change in perspective helps release the 'stuck story.' To embrace a new awareness allows for an expansion in your corner of the universe. Each generation builds on the previous generation. We were all given a set of beliefs, and definitions of 'right' and 'wrong,' 'good' and 'bad' from our parents or guardians. Part of the process of evolution or growth is the redefinition of the old paradigm, and the rediscovery of what was previously simply taken for granted as a fact.

In the experience of *The Chocolate Fast*, we are given the opportunity to embrace chocolate and release our own 'stuck story' as it relates to chocolate. We also allow the experience of embracing something fully to work its magic on us completely. When we surrender to the Bliss this act of embracing can create, there is a part of us that understands on a deeper level that Bliss is in fact our birthright.

What if we were to embrace our whole selves? What if we stopped the self-judgment stopped the labeling of right and wrong? What would happen if we chose to allow ourselves to experience Bliss in our lives? What if we could find Bliss in every experience, even the hurt and the pain? What if we could remember that we know, deep down, that Bliss is the underlying message, that Bliss is the natural state of ALL things, and that everything else is the attempt to remember it?

Angel Sigil

ABAHANA

Bring some awareness into your eyes. Open and close them a few times. Take a moment to let your eyes stray from this page and notice something that is far away.

Now look far to the right with just your eyes, and back to center.

Now look far to the left and back. Take this moment to gaze high above your head using your eyes only.

Now move your vision low, again without moving your head. Let your consciousness now rest gently on this page and see if you can notice yourself looking at this book, as if you were witnessing the act as an observer. See yourself see these words.

Now take a deep breath in as if through your eyes and exhale to relax all tension in your eyes and around them. Your eyes are now rested and revitalized for their journey…

Chapter 4

Receiving

Up until now, we have felt so much unconscious guilt that even if we come to understand that chocolate is really very good for us, we still can't let ourselves FULLY enjoy it.

> *It is such an immense relief when you can rid yourself of any guilty feelings. The main thing is not to inhibit the senses, so you can appreciate chocolate one hundred percent. (Chocolate: A Bittersweet Saga of Dark and Light)*

I love this quote, the idea that the guilt is actually inhibiting our senses, our tactile ability to appreciate on every level the experience of chocolate. Think about this for a moment. When we are fully open to something, what does that mean? All senses are go. Right? Our eyes are able to see, our ears to hear, our nose to smell, our tongue to taste and our body to feel. From a yogic standpoint, these 5 senses contain deeper wisdom; the sense organs are known as jnana-indriyas or 'organs of knowledge.' This means that we don't only see with our eyes, but through them we have a deeper capacity to see—an inner vision. When our body is clear, our mind is open, and we can tap into this layer of sensation, this wisdom. Some call this level of vision clairvoyance. The same is true with our ears: we have a deeper capacity to hear what is present beyond what our ears can pick up (clairaudience). We have what is sometimes referred to as the 'sixth sense'—another kind of knowing, deeply intuitive in nature. In yoga, the sixth sense is believed to operate at the 'third-eye' or forehead center, through which we receive these intuitive promptings and inspiration. There is even a deeper capacity available to us called Omni-sensory perception, where we can actually experience all the senses through any and every sense organ. (Let this idea settle in for a moment...)

When we feel guilt or any other distressing emotion (fear, shame, depression, etc.) we block our ability to 'sense'—not just the flavor of the chocolate, but all the layers of reality that are potentially available to be experienced, including Bliss.

Most people feel so much unconscious guilt, that even if Bliss were placed in their hands, they would shrink, or drop it and run away from it. Perhaps this is what is meant by the 'consuming flames of hell.' We create our own hell by our state of mind and through our stuck stories. I believe it is the distressing emotions we become attached to that disallow us the experience of Bliss or God, they so consume us. We shrink from the Bliss out of our own feelings of unworthiness.

What do we believe collectively about Bliss? That we are undeserving? That Bliss is only attainable after we die—in heavenly realms?

What do we believe collectively about chocolate? What is the underlying feeling? We love it, we want it—but we feel guilty for wanting it. Most of us continue to believe that chocolate is bad for us, don't we? Part of us even wants it to be bad, I think. Consider, for example, how much positive research is today being published about the health benefits of chocolate. Yet when we read about it, it is not without a derisive chuckle under the breath, smacking almost of disbelief. It's as though we don't want it to be good for us; we are perversely attached to the notion that in eating chocolate we are doing something 'unhealthy' or 'sinful.'

Maybe this phenomenon of attraction to the sin, to the 'bad' is what happens to childhood taboos when we grow up. It is our (childish) way of finally winning in the end, doing that thing we were told not to do as a child. Our mothers never knew that one day science would be telling us that chocolate was good for us, so we no longer have to hide behind this label of 'bad' and eat with guilt and shame. Why resist when we can simply embrace? Eat without guilt and shame!

Okay, so perhaps it is not just as easy as making the choice. What if we begin by understanding how the mind works and how our earliest education has translated into every area of our lives? There is an expression "what you resist persists." When we fight a situation, a habit, a feeling, the object of our resistance only gets stronger. Why is that? Based on the Law of Attraction—recently popularized by the hit movie *The Secret* and the subject of much discussion on Oprah—whatever we put our attention on is what we get more of. The Law states that wherever our attention is, our intention is, and the energy follows. In this case, feeling the need to resist the urge to eat chocolate, the emphasis is on the chocolate, wanting or not wanting is irrelevant. If you don't want to eat it, the correct way to create the situation you desire is to think about something else entirely. But thinking about it in any form only increases the attraction to it. We women already know this!

Consider what happens when—at work or in school, for example—we really don't want to be the one picked to do a particular project? We get picked, right? We think it is just our bad luck, but it is really just the Law of Attraction at work. We are thinking about the project and we are thinking about doing it. We might be thinking we don't want to do it, but we are still giving our attention, focus and energy to it. The law of non-resistance states that when obstacles arise in our path, we must be like the mountain stream that meets a fallen bolder: the stream doesn't try to move the boulder or resist it, it simply goes around it. When we decide that we don't want to eat chocolate, or anything else for that matter, we automatically think about wanting it, and we can't resist it. We have set up an attraction to that food just by putting the focus on not wanting it.

A great example of this law in action is the objective of trying to lose weight. How many of us have tried to lose weight in the last year or two? How many of us succeeded? And if we did succeed, how many were able to keep the weight off? I suspect that those who actually lose the weight are more focused on the vision of the self that they want to become, and less concerned with the idea of removing unwanted fat.

The same is true with health matters in general. How many people do you know who are always sick? They themselves would be the first to tell you that they are always sick. By means of their attention, they prepare the ground for their illnesses. They think it is just their system; that it is in their genes to be sick. And what of those who never get sick? They will also be the first to tell you that they never give a second thought to being sick. They simply don't fear it. Their focus is wellness and a healthy existence.

What if we were to stop seeing the possibility for disappointment and illness? What if we simply did not acknowledge them as an option? If we look at current findings related to the mind/body connection, we would find that what is suggested is that a vigilance of the mind can and does effect change in the body. We need to get beyond the habitual obstacles in the mind. We need to begin to see our current results as just that, results that have come out of our way of thinking.

We think we are 'being good' in avoiding or limiting our intake of chocolate. Are we really? I urge you to check out the index as well as the new book by David Wolfe and Shazzie, <u>Naked Chocolate</u>, to see how more and more research is showing that chocolate is actually good for us. It is, in fact, not responsible for the headaches and acne for which it has been blamed in the past; it is rather the sugars, additives, preservatives, milk products, etc. that are the cause of any and all the negative symptoms or side effects that have been attributed to chocolate.

Our attitude toward chocolate, sadly, is representative of our general attitude toward life and its enjoyment. If we allow ourselves a little bit of chocolate and feel guilty afterward, we tend to do the same with other joys in life. We feel guilty for having a completely Blissful experience and prolonged states of ecstasy, no matter the cause. This attitude is a habit, engendered not as a result of actual feeling but rather of societal conditioning; for if we looked at our feelings when holding up the Blissful experience against mundane day-to-day existence, we could easily identify the more desirable state.

And just to reaffirm what I stated in the second chapter, the Bliss we are talking about is not one of dreamy forgetfulness and irresponsibility, but of a high-vibratory state of connectedness to all existence.

So go ahead! Enjoy!

What if we began to become more conscious of each moment? What if we could change a situation just by changing ourselves? There IS something you can do to help to create new patterns of awareness and new outcomes to previously negative circumstances, beginning with the awareness of our own hearts.

HEART TRUTH

Go ahead and take your awareness to your heart now. Perhaps this is the first time you have become aware of yourself in this way. That's okay. Maybe you are already familiar and regularly work with the practice of bringing your awareness to different parts of your body. In any case, I assure you the technique that follows is so utterly simple and so valuable beyond words that I consider it imperative to let as many people know about it as possible. I am a yogi, as I have mentioned. I practice yoga, and I have been meditating many years. I am familiar with bringing my attention to my heart in various ways. When I learned the following technique taught through a non-profit organization called Heart-Math (see index), I was both pleasantly surprised and positively elated at its simplicity and brilliance. Anyone can do this, and you can do it anywhere. It takes only moments and is phenomenally effective.

Heart-Math is cutting-edge scientific knowledge that demonstrates the heart's potential to change everything within us and around us. Did you know that you have a brain in your heart? Intriguing, right? Did you know that your heart emits a vibrational field that affects everything around it for miles? You would be astounded by the strength of the vibration your very own heart waves emit. (I will not go into too much detail here, but you can find out all the information on-line—see index.) The basic process to follow is when feeling stressed or uncomfortable about something, to take a minute to stop and breathe into your heart space. To do this, imagine that your heart is breathing rather than your lungs, so the air is visualized coming in through the front of your chest and exiting the front of your chest. Do this for a few minutes. Next, begin to bring to mind something or someone, some experience for which you have appreciation. Begin to breathe the image or memory of that person, situation, or thing into your heart space. Do this for a few minutes. If you check in with yourself before and after this exercise you will find that your stress and discomfort levels will almost always have dropped significantly after doing this simple exercise.

Bringing new awareness to your breath, your heart, and just life in general will start a chain reaction of positive change in your life that cannot be stopped. For once you say 'yes' to this awareness in any manner, it is self-perpetuating, and the cycle of growth proceeds forward.

It is only in the resisting that we arrest our growth. Whenever we are willing to take a chance, to believe, to breathe…it is in these moments of surrender we begin to open to something deeper, something more pure and true.

I ask you now to step bravely into a place of possibility, a place that enables you to suspend previous 'knowledge' and 'certainties' long enough to allow potential inspiration into your mind and being. With that thought, we are now ready to introduce the ancient art of fasting. Let's approach this subject together, even if you have fasted before, with a fresh perspective, as if we are learning about it for the very first time.

> *Innocence is always unsuspicious.*
> *- Thomas C. Haliburton*

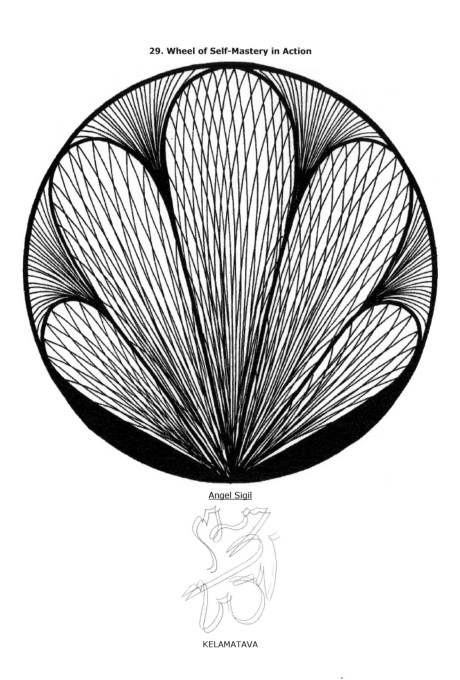

<u>Angel Sigil</u>

KELAMATAVA

Part 2

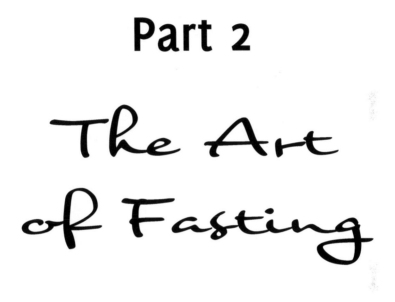

The Art of Fasting

Fasting is the greatest remedy,
the physician within.
- Paracelsus

Feel the length of your spine rising upward from the tail bone to the base of your skull. Notice the life that flows within this vital column even now!

Chapter 5

Remembering

Fasting: v. - Primarily the act of willingly abstaining from some or all food, drink, or both for a period of time. A fast may be total or partial concerning that from which one fasts, and as to the period of fasting, it may be prolonged or intermittent. A complete fast in its traditional definition is abstinence from all food and liquids except water. (Wikipedia)

By definition, fasting occurs outside of one's regular routine. During a fast, your food choices are limited, sometimes to just one item. There is either no selection (i.e. only juice) from which to choose, or very limited choice (i.e. vegetables only) involved. These rules make the experience of fasting not about the food itself so much as about your experience within the fast, and its effects on your body and mind. You become more aware of what is happening in your body when you are not preoccupied with the question of what to put in your mouth. Fasting is a sacred time, a time specially set aside for its purpose alone. It is a time to honor one's body and the act of eating in ways one usually does not. It is a ritual of sorts to be undertaken regularly in order to cleanse the body and the mind, as well as to revitalize our awareness of the beauty and joys of food and eating.

Fasting is often recommended in today's holistic approach to health and wellness as part of a detoxification program. But fasting is nothing new; it has for centuries been an important part of nearly every major religious and spiritual practice in the world. Within these diverse traditions, fasting is unanimously considered to be a way to bring oneself closer to one's true Source.

In the Bible we read of figures such as Moses and Jesus, who both fasted for extended periods of time. In the Far East, Buddha underwent similar fasts, as did other spiritual figures of various traditions. The ritual of the fast continues to be performed today by those seeking to reach finer states of awareness, either of their physicality or of their spiritual nature. Usually it is the case that the refined awareness of both aspects is attained. Fasting is a practice of purification of the mind. It is believed—and experience bears out this belief—that when the body is freed from the 'impurities' of food, the spirit becomes more accessible. Without food we find that we are not just the physical body, but we are…more. We often make the casual mistake of believing that without food we would perish or 'starve to death'. (And for most of us, abstaining from food beyond a certain point, this is true.) But we are composed of so much more than 'food,' than brute matter. Quantum physics agrees: of much finer materials are we made than merely what we can see. In fact, if you break us right down to our most basic 'parts' we are not physical at all, but light molecules—energy. To go one step further from the quantifiable, it is now being proposed that we are ultimately just patterns of information or fields of intelligence.

As the body is freed from the burdensome processes of digestion and assimilation, we are released from the restrictive behavior and the 'slavery' of food. This statement may make all you food lovers cringe, but I invite you to follow this train of thought a little deeper, beyond our culinary enjoyment of food and the animal need to fill the emptiness in our gut. How often do we think about what would really happen if we didn't eat for some time? In more ways than one, we are addicted to the food we consume. But I believe there is something deeper than this explanation. I believe that on some level we are all aware of the ability we have to access those finer layers of our being known as spirit. Those whom we revere as 'conscious beings' and prophets are praised for their ability to live from within a refined, spiritual awareness; and yet we all, I am firmly convinced, have the ability to live in the same manner. The question is: why don't we?

It is a common belief that if you don't eat for a while, you become weak. In terms of the physical body and its development, it is true, bio-mechanically speaking, that you need proteins and calories to build muscle and to provide the tissues with food. But there is a giant part of ourselves we are dismissing with this statement of supposed weakness. There is a life force that flows into us and enlivens our being that is not of physical substance, and without which we do not live. We have already pointed out that, according to research in quantum physics, our 'substance,' such as it is, cannot really be said to be physical. Consider that a human being can live for extended periods of time without food; but without breath—in yogic philosophy, the main vehicle for our life force energy—we would pass on to the next realm in less than five minutes. Even the yogis have learned to slow and even suspend the breath, taking in life-force energy, or *Prana*, by directing their consciousness. Perhaps we have fooled ourselves into believing that we are stronger when focused on the physical rather than on the finer aspects of being. But what if it is the constant reliance on food, on the physical, that is the weakness?

So, then, what happens during a fast besides mere lack of food? Well, for one thing, the voluntary act of ceasing our intake of food. It is a choice of mastery over the body, over the ruling voice of hunger. In that choice lays the potential for empowerment. Anytime you make a choice and stick with it whole-heartedly, an unseen source of power seems to flow into the situation to support your choice. The key word here is 'heart,' for it is in your heart that you hold the vibration that can heal, connect you to your purpose, give you strength and draw in the positive experiences you desire. But in grosser terms, just think about this: day in and day out, your stomach is ruling you. You are a slave to three-meals-a-day (and then some) to keep this body kingdom happy. To voluntarily take the reins, to become the master of when and what enters the body, is an empowering experience not to be looked down upon.

When Moses, Jesus, Buddha, and other lesser-known spiritual figures fasted, they did so with an end in mind. They desired to move beyond the limitations of the body and contact the greater force in existence, the force that enlivened their very being. This is the inherent and ancient energy carried by a fast. We say that we carry the genes from our parents and ancestors for illness and disease. Well, we also carry the even more ancient patterns of knowledge in our cells, the ones that remember who we really are, our essence. Modern DNA tests show that we are literally ALL connected. We hold the memory of fasting in us, and the memory of Self-empowerment through this time-honored ritual act.

So, now let us consider eating only chocolate for a day and look more deeply at the content of this food choice.

As I have previously mentioned, if you look into David Wolfe & Shazzie's recent book Naked Chocolate you will find an amazing list of the nutrients contained within chocolate. (I have included a glimpse in the index) Now, for the most part, this is true of raw chocolate – cacao – more than the processed version. But all chocolate contains the mood enhancing neurotransmitter phenylethylamine (PEA). Phenylethylamine stimulates dopamine (the 'feel-good' hormone) as does theobromine, another constituent of chocolate. And all chocolate contains ananadamide, the bliss chemical. Anandamide is the chemical the body produces during ecstatic states. Ananadamide is the chemical present in the body when you are experiencing Bliss. This is the experience we are seeking to align with in this fast, so what better food choice to take along on the journey? It is built right into the chemical make-up of chocolate to experience Bliss! There is no battle of the wills when choosing to eat only chocolate for a day. Rather, I think instead it feels like a cheat, a blessing, a gift, an opportunity. For once you have made the decision to fast on chocolate alone, then it is the intention (as is explored in later chapters) that becomes most important element of the fast.

Isn't it exciting that the food that is a source of guilt and inner conflict in this culture is also a food capable of connecting us with our most natural state of Bliss? Does this seem 'too good to be true'? Perhaps it feels too good, but *halleluiah* that it is also true!

As we approach your *Chocolate Fast*, I encourage you to allow the prospect of remembrance and allowing into your being. For all at once we have the opportunity both to heal the stories that have restricted us in the past as well as to reconnect to our divine essence, all in the simple and beautiful act of eating chocolate for a day.

Become aware of your body and the many parts of your body which are touching the surface (the chair, bed, wall or floor). Notice the weight of those parts. Let your consciousness move into each one of these points for just a moment. Feel yourself sinking into the body even more. Notice how you are supported. Perhaps as you become aware of your position you feel the need or desire to change it. Adjust as you feel moved to. Once again notice these contact points. Imagine you could breathe in through them for a moment…

Feel yourself relaxed and supported in your chosen position.

Chapter 6

Relaxing

Most of us eat a minimum of 3 meals a day, every day of our entire lives without giving it much thought. (And let's not forget to include our intake of medications—they count as food, too—and of course, dessert!) When I say 'without much thought,' I am not saying that we don't enjoy eating—some of us enjoy it so much that it has become one of the reasons we get up in the morning. I am merely suggesting that we don't think of regularly 'not eating' as an option, except in the terms of dieting. And dieting is not normally a pleasant experience, as most of us can attest.

Many of us get a little less than 2 weeks of vacation a year. We work ourselves to the bone, and barely get time to wind down at night before beginning the day over again. This is truly a lamentable state of affairs. How fortunate for us, then, that a fast is like a mini-vacation: a way to take the focus off your normal everyday affairs and to give some care and relief to every aspect of the self, without spending too much time or money in doing so.

When we fast, we are tapping into a state of presence and awareness we that we rarely have the opportunity to enjoy. Why? Well, first of all, many of us avoid fasting for the obvious reason that it sounds like it could amount to a pretty uncomfortable experience. And let's face it—many of us have difficulty finding time for a 'retreat' of any kind.

We live in a fast-paced world; we are used to instant results. Instant coffee, fast food, express lanes, instant messaging, direct deposit...it must be quick, quick, quick! We get upset when we have to wait for the results we want. It's the same thing with our health and our quest for spiritual fulfillment: we want the wonder pill, or the "lose weight while you sleep!" program; we seek the lightning path to "Universal Oneness" and want to be 'redeemed' right now. Believe me I can relate! In my own quest for the fast track to enlightenment I have found perspective to be imperative. I have learned that if we can begin to implement a subtle 'shift' in our individual and collective perspectives we will begin to find that the Bliss is always there, waiting to be experienced... and that instant gratification isn't necessarily false, but instead you could say that we've been looking in all the wrong places... outside rather than in. So how do we make the shift?

Computer programmers have a saying: Garbage in, garbage out. What goes in—what we put into our bodies, what we put into our minds—must come out. We eat our food, and we must release what we have consumed. We take in a belief (consciously or unconsciously) and it is brought out again, either robotically or applied with awareness. I am quite sure if we were all sitting in a room together having this discussion we would be in agreement, for this seems basic.

What if you could approach fasting, or anything in life, with the attitude of 'what if,' rather than with a set of assumptions about what is supposedly known? The person who would not have considered fasting before, basing her decision on the supposed or even documented possibility of physical unpleasantness, could decide to fast as an experiment [note: the French word for experiment is experience...] of self: to perhaps test the limits and journey into what has previously been unknown to and about herself. I believe a willingness to take a risk in order to 'see the bigger picture,' to gamble on life and open up to unexpected possibilities, this is what separates those who stagnate in life from those who move forward, evolve, achieve. The willingness to experience the unknown, to move through the feelings and discomfort that may come up while fasting, that willingness will get you to the other side of them where you will reap the true harvest that a fast has to offer: clarity of mind, increased energy, improved digestion and memory, better skin tone, clearer eyes, more self-belief and confidence, increased will power, spiritual connectedness, centeredness and a quiet mind. Wouldn't all that be worth a little discomfort?

Let us think for just a moment about what happens in the body when the steady intake of nourishment is arrested. Imagine you are one of the organs in your body—say, the liver. The liver has over 500 jobs in the body. Of those 500+ jobs, one of its major jobs is detoxification. Over 2 quarts of blood pass through the liver, through you, every minute for purposes of detoxification. This filtration of toxins is absolutely critical, as the blood coming from the intestines contains high levels of 'bad' bacteria, and a variety of other toxic substances. If you—the liver—are working properly, you clear over 99 percent of these toxins in the first pass through your amazing self. This is just phase one of your detoxification process. You also produce bile (approximately 1 quart a day) to be dumped into the intestines for removal from the body. The third phase involves an enzymatic process to neutralize unwanted chemical compounds.

Not only do you quarantine and breakdown physical toxins, but you are the storehouse for all the hormonal compounds associated with the body's emotions. A large amount of unexpressed emotions are stored here, in hopes of the chance to be released one day. So, when the food intake drops down to nearly zero, and instead, large amounts of water, herbal tea and an unparalled antioxidant-rich substance (ie. chocolate) show up, what do you do? I imagine you would take a deep, free breath, and then sigh with relief. Next, you would look around yourself, finally able to notice all those toxins that have been building up, too poisonous to release into the body during regular hours of operation, and proclaim: "I think it's time to clean house!"

This is the reaction of all your organs when presented with the opportunity to relax from performing their normal duties. For most of us, especially those who have never taken any kind of a break from eating, it is likely that we have a lot of toxins stored up. The nice thing about making chocolate the substance of your fast, is that those amazing hormone-producing chemicals in chocolate induce a positive mood and a Blissful state. What better friend could you have along with you while 'clearing the clutter' from your inner house?

The next chapter we go further into the idea of 'clearing the clutter'. Before we go there, let's once again revisit the idea of opposites. What goes in must come out. Food, emotions, ideas/ beliefs, this is a constant process. Do you think we could ever reach the point where what comes in and what goes out are relatively balanced? And if so, what would that look like? What changes would need to take place within you in order to make the negative emotions and experiences of your life into positive ones?

30. Wheel of Self-Seeing Perfection

Angel Sigil

ARUGALAHARA

Draw in a nice slow deep breath through your nose. Exhale through your nose. Do it again, but this time see if you can pause at the top of your breath, and hold it in, just for a brief moment. Do the same at the bottom of your breath when your body is void of air. Feel the emptiness before the filling.

Chapter 7

Releasing

Along with the release of physical toxins from the body comes the ability to release old thought patterns and to make space for new, more empowering ones. Fasting is a space-maker, an excavator, a spiritual digging machine. When you stop the continuous intake of the habitual and allow a 'draining' or 'clearing,' so to speak, you make room in the body and mind for more energy, more life, and a healthier you.

On a physical level, you may experience a loss of weight. On a mental level, the space opened by 'draining' holds a new sense of energy, of passion returning and creativity emerging. As for all of the old ideas you were holding onto that you weren't doing anything with (and that weren't serving you anyway)—all this 'dead' weight is released with the cleanse. A sort of vacuum state is produced within the mental field that acts to draw in the fresh, new creative energy.

For many, the process of clearing that happens during a fast can be somewhat intense. It is therefore recommended that you reserve the entire day for yourself. Pick a day that you can dedicate to the fast and completely focus on enjoying and pampering yourself.

The body, in its regular digestive processes, is constantly removing and storing chemicals and harmful substances. Along with the toxic foods, emotions that we cannot handle at the time they are triggered are also stored there. When these feelings are not expressed, they become more toxic. As food wastes are evicted from the temple of the body during fasting, the body can also begin to release stagnant stored emotions. Fasting is a way of relaxing the organs and body tissues, giving them a break from their regular routine. In relaxation comes release. We've all experienced those twitches in our muscles during deep rest, a symptom of unwinding; the same dynamic holds true during fasting, only more intensively. A stored emotion is a tension in the body that was unable to be processed and 'released' at the time it was created. When we relax muscles, the stuck emotions are able to shake loose and come out. When we let our organs relax, they release too!

At the time of an unprocessed emotional trigger, our bodies hold the repressed emotion in the tissues most associated with the action we were performing. In many cases these occurrences take place during food consumption, and therefore our digestive system is compromised. Here is an example of how emotional 'clots' can occur.

Say you are just about to sit down for dinner with roommates, when the phone rings. You pick up the phone, only to receive the news that you have been dumped! Aargh! You are emotional, of course, but you want to remain calm and sit down with your roomies to eat anyway because you don't want to cause a scene or disrupt their meal. Much of the emotion that really needed to come out right away gets swallowed with your dinner. Sound familiar? The emotions you 'didn't' have are now stored as toxins. Later, when you go to your room, you feel sick. And no wonder: the food you have eaten has been rendered toxic by association with the feelings of rejection and pain you are experiencing.

(Next time, skip the dinner, go outside and throw some rocks at your fence, shoot some hoops, scream—let it out! Then, you can return to food or other activities without the toxic side effects.)

As I said, to fast is to 'clear the clutter.' It is quite common for suppressed emotions to surface or be 're-experienced' as they are being released. It is normal—but not obligatory—to feel the urge to cry, for example, or get angry, for what seems like no reason at all. These responses are the body's throwing off of the previously suppressed emotion. It is important to remember this possible side effect so as not to blame your current life situation for any emotional upwelling you might experience. Rather, rejoice that those feelings are coming out now instead of staying inside you any longer with the potential of manifesting later as more serious disease.

To fast means basically to quit eating (normally) for a time. This act of 'quitting' eating activates our inner will power. Many of us believe we have a weak will power. How many of us have tried to diet or fast before and failed? I know I have. Why do we fail? Our desire for the 'good tastes,' for immediate gratification, wins out over our desire for the end result, does it not? But we can remedy this battle with desire through *The Chocolate Fast*. First of all, in this fast we are only eating the dessert—the food that so often derails our commitment to a diet in the first place. It is the perceived enemy we are embracing, here; and since it is these 'food enemies' that usually vanquish us in our efforts, this fast should be a piece of cake, literally and metaphorically speaking!

When you embrace the fast by eating only chocolate, you have still embraced the fast. You can do it, because it seems more to the conscious mind like a win (the best of both worlds), even like a cheat. Still, you have trained yourself to fast. You have taken yourself out of the regular routine of eating for an entire 24 hours. All of your body's systems will thank you for the much-needed break. You will possibly even feel wonderful from the added happy hormones during the process (thanks to the chocolate), and you will be even happier to return to the healthy foods that you weren't so keen on eating as faithfully before. It is a triple win!

When we fast we set a specific goal—we have guidelines and intended results. When we become detailed with our vision for our life (remember: the mind works with pictures and images), life will more accurately reflect the energetic blueprint we have set before it. Remember, wherever we put our attention and intention is where the energy goes. Engaging in this fast, you are creating an experience for yourself that is specific, with specific results in mind. Our intention is to tap into the Bliss of who we are through the experience of eating chocolate.

Take just a moment to feel your lips. Did you automatically lick them when your attention went there? Do they feel dry, wet? Is there a lingering flavor at their corners? Notice any possible tightness in your lips and consciously allow them to relax. Mmmm!

Chapter 8

Intending

This is worth repeating: *The Law of Attraction* says that the mind is a magnet and attracts whatever corresponds to its ruling state. The classic example: If I tell you not to think of a pink elephant right now, what do you think of? You can't help but to think of the pink elephant, that is where your attention was drawn to. The mind or imagination cannot be directed not to think something, and attention draws attention. Your intention is the same: if you intend and set out to cross a bridge by car, is it likely you would find yourself on your bike in a field? No. If you get on a plane that is bound for Canada, do you worry that you will end up in Texas? No. Because where the intention is, that's where the energy and experience follow. Now emotions are a little more tricky, as are mental states, sometimes when we intend to feel a certain way, or think a certain thing, the situation we find ourselves in often 'seems' to cause us to respond in a way other than how we 'intended' to respond. Bear in mind, however, that when you do take the time to set an intention, you have a much greater opportunity to experience that which you intend, and the things that are keeping you from experiencing that which is intended has more to do with previous programming and mental conditioning than it does with the intention. For, as many of us who have been working with mind/body medicine and affirmations can attest, the more you set the same intention – repeating the desired result – again and again, the greater the likelihood of experiencing what you desire. Again, cellular memory!

So, when you intend to clear the body, experience your true state of abiding Bliss in association with a diet of pure chocolate, the probability is great (and gets greater every time) that you will in fact experience that very thing. We create what we intend. We are creative beings, and we cannot help that we are co-creators of our life: we can only help what we are creating, by our intention. Think about how we normally consume. We usually choose to fill our shopping cart full of the foods we habitually buy. To choose new foods, even for a day, is to design a different sort of experience: it is the intention to experience something new.

I remember the first time I observed a three day juice fast. I was at the grocery store filling my cart with the items I would need for the three days—3 gallons of grape juice, 3 gallons of distilled water, a pint of olive oil and 48 ounces of prune juice— and psychologically, just standing there in line with all this in my cart, something started to shift inside me. I had taken the necessary initial steps toward creating change in my body and in my life, and the changes had already begun.

The intention inherent in the process of fasting is probably the most important aspect of the experience. When you undertake a fast, you are choosing to choose what will be going into your body for the duration of the fast…ahead of time! Our bodies are highly intelligent organisms, right down to each and every cell. In brief, when we know what we are going to do and we actively think about it ahead of time—write it down, follow a formula—we are setting an intention, and our bodies really like that. They know what to expect—they know how to handle it, because they have forewarning.

It has been explained to me that one of the reasons it is customary in places like India and Morocco, for example, to eat with one's hand(s), is that the hands are an extension of the digestive system. Really! Your fingers have so many nerve endings in them that they begin to relay the message of the food—its temperature, spice content, etc.—to the body before it even enters the mouth, so the body can anticipate its arrival and thus have the proper digestive juices ready for whatever is being consumed. Isn't that brilliant?

The same principle is at work in the decision to fast. When you make the choice to do this chocolate fast, you are, in essence, telling your body what to expect for the twenty-four hours that you are engaged in it. You are allowing your body to prepare itself for what you will be giving it. When you fast according to this method, you become more conscious about what you put in your mouth, and you approach each bite as a sacred offering to the digestive fires. In this way, each morsel that you consume becomes a representation of your desire to experience a finer state, to contact your natural state of being—Bliss—beyond this human form. As we are coming to understand, chocolate is more than just its delicious self. Chocolate is a metaphor for our Bliss, as well a literal creator of Bliss in the body. Moreover, chocolate is a vehicle, through the Fast, for making contact with our greater Self.

When we return to our 'regular' diet after a fast, we are bound to see food in a whole new light. Perhaps because we have allowed all of its essence to leave our form, and invited a cleansing to take place, the return to everyday consumption does take on an element of novelty that was absent before the fast. Personally, this new beginning is one of my favorite parts of fasting. For we so often take the food that gives us strength for granted. We eat, day in and day out, forgetful of the miracle and the blessing that it is. When we fast for even twenty-four hours, and then begin the day after to approach food again, we cannot help but see it in a new light, treating it with more honor and respect. One could express this simply as a return to the joy of eating again, and there is that.

But it is awesome to think of how we regained that joy, which only two days before had to some extent been lost over the years through unmindful repetition of the act of filling one's belly.

Within the time frame set aside for the fast, we are really brought into a new relationship with the food we consume, and ultimately with all food. The act of eating becomes more about the moment and the taste in that moment than about what is to follow (the next course, the dessert, going back to work, going to work out, etc). We have the opportunity to become more aware of what is happening in our mind and in our body when we are not so consumed with what happens next.

31. Wheel of Compassionate Understanding

Angel Sigil

HELIMA-HAKA

Part 3

Tilling
the Soil

Imagine you have a string that runs up the center line of your body, from the base of your spine up through the top of your head, and that you are being suspended by it. Notice if you feel more weight or awareness on one side or the other. See whether, just by virtue of your awareness, there isn't a balancing out that begins to take place between the two halves of your body, between your two minds.

Chapter 9

Aligning

Modern science reveals that we are nothing but vibrating molecules of energy. We know that the higher something's vibrational state, the more alive it is. In human beings, lower vibration is related to states of dis-ease. In other words, health is the result of our cells vibrating faster, or at a higher frequency. When we feel good, we are feeling that higher vibration.

When we are feeling really great, we are aligned with our life's purpose, or simply, with Life. Life itself is vibrating within us. We are able to live well when we feel good, and thus are able to do what we are drawn to do. When we feel 'bad' or low in our body or 'about' something, this feeling is a form of communication from our body telling us that that whatever we are contemplating or whatever we are experiencing does not bring us Life—it is not in alignment with our life essence, it is not part of what propels us to live. Does that make sense? In another way: Whatever makes us feel good, that feeling confirms to us that our thoughts and actions are in alignment with our life purpose, with Life itself.

Many books have been written on the subject of the power of our thoughts and emotions. Louis Hay's <u>You Can Heal Your Life</u> was one of the first such books I remember reading, and remains one of my favorites. This book teaches us about the power of thought and affirmations. These truths have been revealed in thousands of ways in every spiritual teaching, and by numerous authors throughout written history. Even today, science is revealing—and the modern medical establishment agrees—that how we feel affects our experience in every realm of life: physical health, mental and emotional well-being, and spiritual connectivity. Those who are sick with cancer or other terminal illnesses can adopt a positive, loving and grateful attitude and completely heal from their illness. I've seen it happen on more than one occasion. This kind of "miraculous" self-healing is a very real phenomenon.

A good friend of mine was diagnosed with terminal colon cancer at age 29. The doctors gave him two months to live and advised him that surgery would not be beneficial or extend his life much, if at all. At this news, my friend fell into a downward spiral of despair and self-pity. Normally of a fit, lean physical disposition, after the diagnosis and time spent wallowing in depression he gained a lot of weight and began to look really terrible. It wasn't until after his "two months to live" had expired that he let on to anyone of his illness. I was the only person he told at the time, and only on the condition that I would let him die in peace and with dignity. Being the 'natural healing junkie' that I am, my inclination was to get him onto some cleanses and help him to heal. But that was not the path he was ready to take.

It wasn't until he landed himself in Hawaii—his chosen spot to pass on—and happened to meet a woman who was healing herself from a chronic condition that his life began to turn around. You see, he had gambled with fate, and taken only enough money for a few days, thinking his end was so near. When he ran out of money, his ego prevented him from calling anyone he knew for help, so he accepted the invitation of this angel to stay with her for a bit. Her invitation was not without conditions. She informed him that he could not stay unless he adopted the attitude of one who would live, not one who was in despair and dying. He was given the ultimatum of all ultimatums: 'Choose life, or be abandoned on the streets to die alone.' He chose life. From that day on, with a newfound will to live, everything in his body and health turned around. He immediately began to heal, and within six months he was completely cancer free. That's not to say it was all smooth sailing, but he will tell you that the most important part of his ability to heal was his mental attitude, his surrender to a higher power, and surrounding himself with others who believed he could heal. That is where I got to be a part of his life again. He is a good friend still today, and as enthusiastic a proponent of the power of positive thinking as you will ever meet—and with good reason!

Mind-body experts have discovered that cancer can result from harbored anger or other strong repressed emotions, and diabetes from not allowing oneself to experience the 'sweetness' of life. In this regard, Louise Hay's book is an excellent resource: you can look up any physical condition and find the corresponding emotional states, including affirmations to assist in changing those beliefs and healing. Like increasingly many other practitioners of the 'alternative' healing arts, I have found it to be true that whatever we believe is true for us—what EVER we believe.

While reading these words, let your awareness move into your right foot. Without looking at it, feel as though it is starting to get bigger and bigger with each breath. Your right foot is expanding to become twice its normal size; all of your breath is going to your right foot.

Now transfer your attention to your left foot and feel it expanding, growing, inflating, enlarging, becoming bigger than ever.

Now feel that you—all of you—is increasing in energetic size to agree with your feet.

Now feel how much larger are you and your life than they were only moments ago!

Chapter 10

Expanding

Our brain is a processing machine: an organic computer, if you will, that uses hormones to send messages to the body. Our emotions are all a result of hormones. Our cells can be happy or sad. How do they come to be happy or sad? Well, the cells in our body actually respond to what we think. Our brain tells the body to produce certain hormones—endorphins, serotonin, dopamine, anandamide, etc.—which in turn make us feel great. A lack of these hormones, or too much of them, contribute to depression, anger, irritation and other 'not so great' feelings. Our senses are jacked right into this electro-chemical feedback machine called the brain. What happens when we are assaulted by the stench of rotting garbage, or open the kitchen compost to catch an unwelcome glimpse of larva spilling out of the fruit peels? I know, disgusting right? That shock, no matter how 'mild,' triggers the release of cortisol from the adrenals into the bloodstream. Cortisol gives a quick burst of increased immunity in presumably 'threatening' situations. If the stimulus is revolting enough, you might get a little adrenaline out of the bargain, as well.

Concurrent with this 'hormonal party' within the body, we may notice (through a subtle shift of attention) changes in our energy field: an expansion or contraction happening within and around us. What is it that occurs energetically during this same experience of 'shock' or disgust? Let's look at what happens when we take a bite of something rotten. Our whole body system responds: it contracts. Eating something pleasing, on the other hand, creates an expansion of our energy field and a 'Yes!' in the brain and the cells of the body (those happy hormones at work). The only way a 'yes' tasting food can change into a 'no' in the body and cells is if you add to it your judgment or condemnation. If, for example, you say something like, "This is amazing food, too bad it's bad for me", you counteract the expansion that the taste gave you on every level. Since your brain is obedient, and believes you, automatically, the food actually becomes "bad for you" instead of the "amazing" experience your taste buds first dictated.

Let's not confuse food addiction with true response. You can be addicted to sugar, or caffeine or various substances, and when that substance touches your lips and gets into your blood stream you can feel that systemic sigh of relief. This is not the same as the true feeling of awe in the body, that response to something absolutely extraordinary touching your tongue. Recall to yourself the most delicious, fulfilling dessert you ever experienced. You know it isn't a Snickers bar or a Twinkie, or some other sugar fix. Perhaps it was Grandma's apple pie when you were a child. Grandma's pie was also made with love; we felt that energy when we ate it.

If you love and enjoy doing something, it brings you joy and health and is of a high vibration. It expands you. Stated another way, what makes you feel good gives you the sensation of expansion. But if you dislike doing something, if you dread it, you are experiencing a lower vibration, or contraction.

Think about someone you love—a child, a lover—and feel how you experience expansion in that thought of love. Experience the Life and the sense of purpose those thoughts bring you. Now think of a dark alley filled with garbage and potential harm for you and your family. Notice how your energy contracts. Can you feel that? That is the signal of a situation not being in-line with your life purpose. Think of your favorite place in the world, somewhere you like to travel, or a vacation spot. Again, notice the sense of expansion in yourself when you think of that. Now imagine someone yelling at you. Can you feel contraction, shrinking? The way you feel about a situation or person can be viewed as your monitor for knowing if something is in alignment with your purpose. Your purpose is what brings you life; it is what you love, what expands you.

Now these examples are more obvious ones. Not all of our experiences and decisions are so easy or clear. Take the idea of a certain job offer. Let's say you would be getting a nice office space, good pay, friendly co-workers—but not in your chosen field. You would have less vacation time, but more benefits. In this scenario, you might feel expansion in certain areas and contraction in others. What is the overall sense you get when you imagine yourself in this position? That is the question that needs to be answered, remembering that Life flows wherever you feel most expansive.

The Universe moves in an evolving, upward spiral. We are growing, becoming, expanding. Look at the way everything in nature grows: a flower, a tree, upward, toward a greater and greater expression of itself. We are no different.

"You can increase your pleasure four or five times simply by learning how to taste chocolate. When you determine your favorite sorts and styles, it gets even

better. You always know which one will please you the most at any moment. And if you listen, your body will tell you how much you need."

(Chloe, our chocolate expert, remains convinced that fine chocolate will be appreciated, more and more, for its sensual qualities. She sees new attitudes toward chocolate not as some passing wave but rather as a fundamental change.)

"I think growth will be explosive. More and more people will be sensitized. The designations of 'appellation d'origine controlee' will follow the same course they did with wine and then olive oil… How can it be otherwise? Good chocolate brings so much pleasure. And, en plus, it is extremely good for health." <u>(Chocolate: A Bittersweet Saga of Dark and Light)</u>

This depiction of our evolving relationship with chocolate nicely parallels the spiritual process we are undergoing today with respect to our deepening appreciation of a more expansive relationship to the truth of who we really are—our most authentic and powerful nature. To borrow the words of Chloe X, this new experience of ourselves is not a passing wave, but a fundamental change. Chocolate has become a brilliant reflection of how we assess our worthiness to feel joy, and how deserving of true Bliss we believe ourselves to be.

As we evolve this belief and go through the process of self-acceptance, healing and renewal, we see that our relationship with something as deep, dark and rich as chocolate is also able to evolve. We become more able to receive the joy that the experience of chocolate has to offer us. We open ourselves up to the potential to feel the Bliss, minus all the guilt. This is the expansive quality of nature, of our spirit: to seek after greater and greater expressions, emotions, and experiences.

The experience of chocolate as a guilty pleasure pales in comparison to the unabashed celebration of the Bliss that can be tapped when one truly surrenders to the sensation of 'melting at body temperature.' How often to we allow ourselves to, in essence, melt? We often hear the phrase, 'Pull yourself together,' but do we ever encourage one another to 'melt down and open up?'

Relaxation is too undervalued in my opinion. As a culture, we continue to put a very high premium on work and working out. The understanding is that tension is what holds us together. Even in the world of yoga as it is practiced in the West, the intensity with which many of us pursue this path is often something less than relaxing. I know that was my experience when I first started practicing. It wasn't until I went away to India for an intensive yogic lifestyle immersion retreat at a traditional ashram that I was introduced to the idea of relaxation, and how to accomplish it through 'yoga.' I must admit, this notion met with a good deal of resistance on my part. After all, when I got to 'yoga school' I was fit and buff and trim with my muscular vinyasa power yoga body. (I still love vinyasa.) In truth, I was a bit angered when the head Swami—the equivalent of a school principal or business CEO—told me, after hearing of my practice, that he was tired just listening to me and hoped I would take this time to relax. Relax? I came to do yoga! Again, I undervalued what it might mean to my practice to 'relax'. I had not yet considered that relaxing might actually improve and deepen my yoga practice as well as my knowledge and relationship with yoga and myself. The truth is, I did learn to relax. It took some unwinding, yes, and *some* muscle 'mass' loss (a little, not a lot), it took surrendering rather than resisting; but in the end I didn't just 'learn' yoga, I became it.

Is it possible that Bliss has a muscle? An interesting thought. What if it is in the deep relaxation of this 'muscle' that we really begin to experience its strength?

During one meditation at the ashram, I had an interesting experience in which I actually became aware of something equivalent to a 'muscle' of meditation. In the process of my observation, I noticed that this muscle was almost completely atrophied—and completely tense—from lack of use. It had started to loosen, but it was obvious to my meditating mind that I had kept it quite contracted for a very long time, and that it had only just begun to relax and open as I was starting to open myself up to this deeper and deeper allowing. I sensed that in the opening and relaxing of this 'muscle' I would be entering a very expansive state: that of pure consciousness, one that I had perhaps previously feared. When I questioned my fear of what I now know in retrospect to be so desirable to me, I realized that the fear was of the possibility of insanity, or of 'too much' allowing. How can it be that we fear pure consciousness? If pure consciousness is Bliss, as so many who have entered that state describe it, then what is to fear?

This question was first brought to my attention through the practice of Transcendental Meditation, and by the words of Maharishi Mahesh Yogi to the effect that we are used to our awareness being focused on something—after all, we have been working on that since the day we were born. Focusing on mother's face, on a rattle, a finger, the wall, someone entering the room, on colors—and on and on. We come from a state of expansiveness, but when we enter these bodies we are forced to learn how to focus our awareness, and we tend to (over time) forget how to release that focus and return to the experience of pure consciousness -hence the atrophied tension of the 'Bliss-muscle.' We forget our true Bliss—for who would argue that an infant lives in a state of Bliss?

As we grow, we begin at some point to notice our inherent craving for that experience of pure consciousness once again. Often that craving is ignored or misinterpreted and shows up as enormous stress and dis-ease. But even with dis-ease we are merely experiencing a misalignment within our field of focus. We are still, at some level, craving our true nature. When still unrecognized, this misalignment is, I believe, what eventually leads most people to death, where there is a release from the focus back into Bliss, back into the expansive nature of their being. If we cannot receive the awareness of our truth while in this bodily form, if we cannot find a way to accept Bliss here, in our physicality, then we will need to put the flesh aside, for we naturally crave and are drawn toward the Bliss experience that is our truest expression. But what if we can embrace Bliss while in this form…oh, what then are the possibilities?

Perhaps we are getting a little deep now. If so, it is because I feel it is important, before embarking on the journey of this fast, to set the intention toward the highest possible experience. Why aim low, and risk falling right there? Why sell ourselves short, when we really have nothing to lose but our preconceptions of what we can expect from ourselves and from life?

If you bought this book thinking it would be the perfect excuse to eat just chocolate for 24 hours—well, it is that, and now you have your permission to indulge. But if, on some level of your being, you recognize the desire to reach a deeper place within you, to experience greater peace and especially greater Bliss; or even better, if you feel a resonance with the vibration being expressed here, then I invite you to continue on to the many layers that await…of chocolate and You.

32. Wheel of Self-Confidence

Angel Sigil

BLAVEK-KARANEK

Part 4

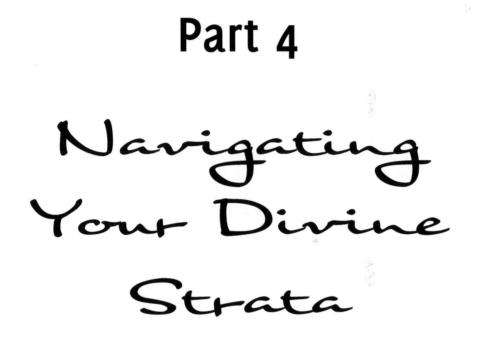

Navigating
Your Divine
Strata

The following story is one that has been told for millennia by the mystics and yogis of ancient India. Its truths are now finally being uncovered by modern science. This is the story of five bodies. I know—you thought you only had one body, right? Well...while it's true that you have only one physical body, but you have at least four other bodies of a more subtle nature. Maybe you have only one physical body, but in actuality you have at least five bodies, most of which are of a more subtle nature. (I am now learning there are as many as 12 – maybe more!) You know of several of these bodies already. One of the ways you know of them is through the experience of chocolate; so it makes sense in this context to relate each layer or each body to the aspect of chocolate to which it correlates.

Become aware of your entire body as if from the outside. Imagine that you are gazing upon yourself now in your seated position. See yourself, without judgment, from all sides. Walk around your body mentally. Observe your posture. Notice how your breath moves your body. Notice the shape and dimensions of your body.

Now see if you can notice the more subtle energies. Bring some attention to the space just surrounding your physical body—is there anything there? How does it feel?

Chapter 11

Embodying

The impact is physiological. Before you start eating it…
your body is already making more phenyl ethylamine, and
then you bite into it, your hypothalamus is stimulated and
sends yet more phenyl ethylamine into the body. You're
in mild shock. (Chocolate: The Bittersweet Saga)

*T*his is an easy one. Reach with one of your hands and touch a part of your body. Congratulations! You are touching your physicality! You wake up into your physical body every day. You wash it, dress it, and feed it. Your body is your vehicle for communicating with the outside world. You place a physical piece of chocolate on your physical body tongue. You feel it melting in your physical mouth. Its mantra is "Yum!"

Our body is a powerful vehicle of force and action. We depend on our physicality to survive and thrive in this physical world. For many people, it is the whole of what makes up human-ness—

it is the totality of experience, it is the sole way of identifying self. It is easy to see why this would be. We look in the mirror and what do we see? We see our self as a body. We look down at our arms, our hands holding this book...We use our bodies day in and day out to perform countless tasks, and yet many would argue that identification with the physical body is our greatest stumbling block to realizing our highest potentials. Could that be the case?

It isn't hard to argue 'what you see is what you get' when the evidence of the senses is so overwhelming. Especially as concerns chocolate, holding the bar is the precursor to the experiences that follow... And that's just it: our experiences too often follows the lead of the obvious, 'in your face' physical realities.

When we peer into ourselves (metaphorically, of course), we can feel something more, that we are something more, and we participate in a more expansive reality than that afforded by our limited physicality. The physical body seems simply to be an outlet for the expression of finer bodies and deeper layers of being.

Say 'Mmmmmm'... and now 'AHhhhhhhhhh'...
How about 'Ooooooohhhhhhh?'

Take just a moment and become aware of any emotions you might currently be experiencing...happiness, bemusement, doubt, fear, wonder, silliness, stillness? Give yourself permission to experience whatever is coming up. Notice it. Validate it. These feelings are there to serve you in this moment. They are an expression of your body interacting with energies within and around you.

Chapter 12

Feeling

Respect for life, truth and patience are all indispensable factors in the drawing of a quiet breath, in calmness of mind and firmness of will.
-Yehudi Menuhin

The second body is an energy body, seen by some as the auric field. This body is what yogis of old called the pranic /energy/ breath sheath, or *pranamaya kosha*. Another name for this field would be the 'emotional body,' as it is largely our emotions and feelings (along with our breathing) that affect this body. You can sense your energy body in its contraction and expansion. When you are feeling ill, depressed, angry, fearful, or even shy, the energy is of a lower vibration and seems to contract or cling close to the body. Your breath, when in these states, is often shallow, tight, or strained. When you are feeling more alive and full of joy, peace, happiness and health you can feel your energy as a higher vibration that seems to reach out from the body or expand. The breath becomes fuller, deeper, richer and more energizing.

The mantra of this body is 'So-Hum'...the sound the breath makes on the inhale and exhale.

Let's once again do a little experiment to see if you can feel this body. Imagine being somewhere in nature that you love—on the ocean, in a forest, near a river. Visualize your surroundings and take a deep breath in… Can you sense either an expansion or contraction in your energy or mood? I'm guessing you can. Now imagine going into the bank and hearing one of the tellers inform you that your account is overdrawn. How is your breathing now? What is your sense of energy? Contraction?

The energy body, in a normal balanced state, reaches approximately two feet around the physical body in all directions, like an etheric eggshell. In chocolate, it is the essence or vibration of the chocolate that directly affects our energy field when we consume it. You could even point to the energy that went into the creation of the chocolate. What were the thoughts and emotions of those picking the beans, melting the cacao butter and adding the sweetener? This might seem like a stretch, but if you consider that we add a piece of our energy to everything we touch, then begin to imagine everything you consume as a means of merging (on some level) to those individuals and energies associated with the creation of that food. With this thought in mind, would you begin to make different food choices? How does the energy of fast food compare with the energy of moms home cooking?

We can begin to feel how even before the release of hormones, after the piece of chocolate hits the mouth we begin to merge with the energy, the life force of chocolate. As the physical chocolate melts it lends us its 'essence' or sensual nature. Our favorite chocolate expert, Chloe Doutre-Russel, explains this phenomenon best:

> "Everyone, no matter who, associates chocolate with the best part of childhood", Chloe said. "Pronounce the word, and people become kids again. It is something precious, a reward. It is warm and humid, and when it melts in your mouth, it inspires a sense of well-being. Just receiving the box, you're already prepared for the experience. Somebody cares about you. Even before you smell the chocolate, you're in a high state of excitement and sensuality because your body has kept the memory of past pleasures."
> (Chocolate: A Bittersweet Saga of Dark and Light)

33. Wheel of Self-Acceptance

Angel Sigil

RENOFLEK

What memory arises when I say the word 'clown?' How about 'rose'?

Bring to mind now the image of the sunset over the ocean. Breathe into this image.

Notice if a particular memory is associated with this ocean scene. Just let the thoughts arise if they are there…

Now bring to mind a pink cloud…a red triangle….a blue star….

You can see these images in your mind's eye, can you not?

Taking a nice deep inhale breath, on the exhale imagine releasing all of these images and breathing in something that makes you very happy.

……hmmmmmmmm……..

Chapter 13

Reasoning

"Free your mind and the rest will follow…"
-En Vogue

The third body is the mental body—in Sanskrit, the *manamaya kosha* or 'mental sheath.' This body is much less limited in its territory than the previous two. It can reach as far as your mind will take you. Have you ever thought of someone who lived clear across the country or the world, and then heard from him or her that very day or even hour? Such events occur by way of this mental body, or mental field, if you will. Quantum science identifies this field as the Unified Field or matrix. It is through this field that we can affect our reality. 'As a man thinketh' and 'thoughts are things' are well-known expressions that speak of the power of this field. The universal principle of the 'law of attraction' we have been discussing—recently popularized by the hit movie *The Secret*—works through this mental body. The mental body, when creating images, draws to itself that which is of like vibration—so, whatever we think about, or put our attention on, is what we experience. That is the power of the mental body. We will delve much deeper into this power in the next chapter, but in this first dimension of mind we are most concerned with and aware of basic instinctual needs—food, finding a mate, protection from danger—than we are of attracting life-enhancing elements. On a humbler—but no less significant—level, the mental body also effects changes in the chemical and hormonal balance of the physical brain, thus giving us our feelings. In this way, the mental layer connects with the physical and emotional bodies.

Think of eating a bar of dark chocolate. Now, when you actually, physically ingest chocolate, the chemical phenylethylamine, a stimulant similar to the body's adrenaline and dopamine, enters the system. You may notice that with merely the suggestion or thought of eating chocolate, you already begin to feel wonderful, and a state of fulfillment, pleasure and bliss enters the stage of the mind/body. How is this possible? It is possible by virtue of the incredible power of this mental sheath. It is in this mental layer, which rules cravings, and in this 'body' that we hold patterns and habits both beneficial and detrimental. Much of the mental body is subconscious and out of our conscious awareness.

It is interesting to note that at a biological level, many of our responses at this level of mind seem to stem from the amygdala or 'reptilian brain,' located at the base of our skull, which is responsible for basic 'animal instincts' like fight and flight. The amygdalae are the physical seat of basic ruling emotions such as love, hate, fear, lust and contentment, concerned with fundamental needs such as survival, physical maintenance, hoarding, dominance, preening and mating. Looking at the mental sheath in this light, we can now begin to see it as the level of mind that connects us to our physicality and our experiences as human animals.

When choosing to consume chocolate as suggested in this book (for 24 hours), the mental body may likely respond with resistance, guilt, and self-doubt, for in our subconscious mind we hold onto the memories, voices, opinions and judgments from our conditioning. Our primitive brain may automatically respond by sending out molecules of emotions armed to protect against the perceived threat of a withdrawal of both love and approval, seeing the chocolate as that threat ('if you eat the chocolate someone will be unhappy with you'), and inadvertently denying us our opportunity to experience Bliss.

The mental body has four parts that continuously interact in order to do the jobs required of them:

The first part of this mental body is the instinctive mind (*manas*).

Second, the sense of 'I' or the ego (*ahamkara*).

The third is memory (*chitta*).

The fourth part is the intellectual mind at its most basic (*buddhi*). (The buddhi also has higher faculties related to the next body field).

A brief summary of the four parts of mind would go as follows:

The instinctive mind is the part that asks the questions 'Will this hurt me?' 'Will it make a good mate?' 'Is it food?' The answers to which result in fight, flight or 'friendship.' The sense of 'I' or ego is the part of us that identifies us as separate from everything else. Memory, at this level of mind, is a basic function acting to remind us if we have seen or experienced 'this' before. Memory serves the intellect here, in the decision of whether or not to do 'this.' The intellect is triggered by both instinct and ego. In the decision-making process of the mental body, instinct asks the question of the ego, who then checks with the memory and informs the intellect—who finally arrives at a decision.

When you think of eating chocolate, what are the first thoughts that come to your mind? Think for a moment about any negative beliefs that may arise. Let them surface completely.

It may help to write them down. (It may serve to mention that by the very act of questioning the functions of the mind we are activating the next body or sheath, which is the higher faculty of the mind. It is difficult to separate our layers distinctly, as they are so interconnected.)

When, through examination, you have identified one negative belief pertaining to chocolate, take a moment to ask of it a few important questions. Where did it come from? Who said it to you? Is it an actual memory, or was it triggered by an instinct? Why has it seemed valid up to this point? Finally, does this thought or belief serve you? By 'serve you' I mean, is it beneficial for you to believe it now, or to continue to believe it?

For example, if the thought is "Eating chocolate makes me sick," you might, through investigating this thought, find that your belief comes from your mother (or another parental authority figure). Maybe you recall being told this quite a lot, particularly around Halloween or other candy-laden holidays when an abundance of chocolate was available to you. Note in your adult mind that the same person allowing or even giving you the chocolate was likely to be the one telling you it would make you sick.

Now, this belief might have seemed valid to you up to this point in your life because you may have an actual memory of becoming sick after eating a large amount of chocolate. Or perhaps it has been a belief set in place to simply 'protect' you from experiencing sickness as a result of chocolate consumption. To ask yourself if this thought serves you now, you have to determine whether this is a healthy thought with which to continue forward in your life. "Eating chocolate makes me sick"—is this a positive thought? Some might argue that it is, because it serves to protect one from getting sick. But let's approach the issue from an angle where we acknowledge the law of attraction at work. If we say that doing something—anything—is going to make us sick, then we are actually inviting the opportunity of sickness. It is something on the order of a self-fulfilling prophecy. If we tie the idea of sickness to eating chocolate, we open ourselves up to and even anticipate the experience of being made ill by chocolate. On the other hand, if we want to create a belief with regard to chocolate that serves us, we might choose to begin to believe that 'consciously eating chocolate connects me to my inherent state of Bliss' and see how that belief makes us feel. In this way we can play with the mental body and the thoughts which have in some way 'ruled'.

In chocolate, the mental body is touched by the release of certain chemicals, such as phenylethylamine, dopamine and anandamide -which help to create pleasant & blissful moods in the body/mind. The thoughts one chooses to have during the ingestion of chocolate stimulates this mental field and the mantra is 'Yes!'

Inhale through your nose… Inhale again…
Deeply fill your lungs and being with breath.
Exhale all that you wish to release.
Now what would you replace it with?
….

Bring something to mind right now: A trait, an object, an
experience…..

Think of it right now and bring in the excitement of receiving it. Really
feel it. Experience yourself already in possession of your desire.

Congratulations! You did it! You have it! You are it!

Now feel the gratitude well up within you for receiving. This is the
important part…

Give thanks, with the essence of your entire being, for your receiving!
Rejoice!

Chapter 14

Creating

To a mind that is still the whole universe surrenders.
LAO TSU (Tao Te Ching)

The fourth body is the wisdom body (*vijnanamaya kosha*). This is the field of greater intelligence we begin to tap into when we are able to align our own desires and will with something greater than survival instincts and conditioning. This something greater we might call a 'Higher mind,' or 'God's Will.' Some refer to this field as the 'Mind of God.' This is the higher expression of the mental field. This field exists whether we are aware of it or not. When we are not aware of it, we simply manifest, by default, whatever we are thinking of via the mental body and interpret surprises and synchronicities as miraculous happenings beyond reason. When we are unaware of this sheath, we live at the mercy of the ego, memory and instincts, as well as the unchecked intellect. On the other hand, when we are aware of this field, then our awareness alone enables us to operate on another level. With our 'perceiving the field,' let's say, the field acknowledges our perception and thereby acts accordingly in response to our request. So, when we begin to align ourselves with this force or this field, we become connected to a larger body of knowledge and the flow of intuition increases, the flow of abundance increases, and the ability to manifest expands.

Intuition is the sense, or mental faculty, that is connected to all that is. 'Cosmic consciousness' is another name for this field— one could say it is the layer 'where all the answers exist'. This field is full of all thought, all ideas, all possibilities. When we stop allowing our basic intellect (or reasoning mind) to rule our actions, when we stop creating by default—according to the processes of the four faculties of mind—and start participating in the co-creative process and open up to this field, we start to receive inspiration through this higher mind, or wisdom body. Think of this body as the place we are all drawing from when we create something. A place where all the creativity, ideas, inspiration originate, and all we need do to tap into it is remove the block—the need for logic—that keeps us from experiencing this body of truth.

We might look at this layer of experience as the place we start to touch an 'altered state of consciousness.' To me, this place is where the experience of the divine origins of chocolate—the divine origins of anything, for that matter—begins to enter the picture. When we begin to reach beyond the human mind we contact something greater. Inspiration and wisdom are beyond human reason. If we allow ourselves to open to inspiration or even 'communion' through chocolate, it too can become sacred— as can anything you allow to transcend mundane interpretation.

The case for chocolate as something sacred is not new; it reaches as far back as the origin of the substance itself.

To say a thing is 'Sacred' is a way to describe something that is beyond everyday human experience. It is that moment when all need for description and rigid identities breaks down, when a sense of something more alive, more real emerges for which there are no words, except to say it is so desirable that you wish to have more and more and more.

The wisdom body is this space; it is what leads us to the more, to the connection between our physical experience of reality and the ultimate experience of our highest potential.

In terms of chocolate, it is when we approach it as a possible means of contacting a higher state that chocolate itself becomes a vehicle to something more than a fleeting pleasure. Chocolate, when we allow ourselves to enjoy it fully—its texture, its essence, the way it expresses itself in your being on every level—can become that sacred ambrosia that the myths celebrate, granting us access to the divine paradise within.

The mantra for this body is 'Hmmmmmm'.

34. Wheel of Clarity

Angel Sigil

DRIVIKISHKIT

I am not this body, I am experiencing this body. I am not this name, I am trying it on. I am not this job, I am playing a game. I am Bliss. I am everything at once and everything is me. I am eternity.

I am Bliss. Bliss is all that I am.

Chapter 15

Blissing

The temple bell stops
But the sound keeps coming
Out of the flowers
BASHO

When we are able to receive the inspiration that so graciously flows through the fourth layer of our divine being, we naturally and automatically begin to touch the fifth body, known in Sanskrit as the *ananda-maya kosha*: the Bliss body. This is the field beyond the higher mind, the field the great Master Jesus spoke of when he said it 'surpasseth all understanding.' It is in this field or state that we contact pure Bliss or Ecstasy, the space that enlightened beings, yogis and masters from all traditions call Nirvana, Heaven, Samadhi, and the Eternal Now. It is the teaching of all great Saints and Masters that we are not this physical body, but the experience of Bliss trying to remember itself, trying to express itself. The exciting thing is that, if we so choose, we get to participate in remembering (or re-membering: bringing all pieces of our self back together) while in this body. It does not have to be an experience deferred until after we 'pass on,' as so many believe. No, Bliss was meant for us in this life, while in the flesh. Again, the great Master Jesus told us that the last enemy to destroy was death (1 Corinthians 15:26). What could he have meant by that? Perhaps it means that too often we reserve the experience of pure joy and pure Bliss as something we will obtain later, after we go from this "vale of tears", rather than something we can obtain here and now. We think it the natural course of things that we weren't meant to be 'that happy' here on Earth. On the contrary, pure joy and Bliss is exactly what we are meant to experience now. To 'destroy' death may very well mean just that—to stop the need for dying. At the very least, to stop the need for death in our minds, for NOW is eternally the right time and place for experiencing all that we have the potential to experience. Perhaps, if we contemplate the words of the great Master a little more we might find a deeper truth revealed: the last enemy to destroy is fear (and isn't death our greatest fear?), for fear is truly the death of our spiritual connection and our ability to experience Bliss! So fear not—Bliss!

In this path of Self-remembrance, I like to think that we, in our highest omniscient expression, gave ourselves little clues along the way to trigger the great knowing—and chocolate, for many of us, is one of those clues. How appropriate that one of the constituents peculiar to chocolate has been named *anandamide*, after the Sanskrit *Ananda*, meaning Bliss.

> "A neurotransmitter called anandamide has been isolated in cacao. Anandamide is also produced naturally in the brain. Anandamide is known as the 'Bliss Chemical' because it is released while we are feeling great. Cacao contains enzyme inhibitors that decrease our bodies' ability to breakdown anandamide. This means that the natural and/or cacao anandamide may stick around longer, making us feel good longer when we eat cacao."
> (www.alivefoods.com)

Anandamide is what our brains produce during ecstatic states. This is happy confirmation of the luminous potential that lies before us with this fast!

When seeking for Bliss, I am reminded again and again, that life's simple things – a child's laugh, a blooming flower, a touch, kicking through the autumn leaves, chocolate… these are the keys…those things which bring delight so easily…a smile, confetti, a warm thank you from the heart, building sandcastles… these gifts we gave to ourselves so we would remember to find ourselves again. This is Bliss. This is Bliss!

As divine beings of Bliss, we are naturally inclined to gravitate toward vibrations of our own kind. Chocolate is a gift from the gods, and WE are made of the very stuff of paradise. It is my desire and blessing that, as we consume the gift of the gods, we begin to uncover our own divine origin, layer by wondrous layer.

The mantra for the Bliss body is 'Ahhhhhhhh!'

Part 5

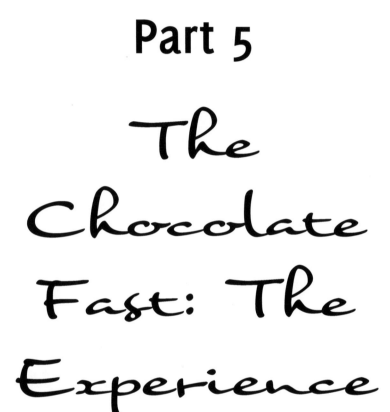

The
Chocolate
Fast: The
Experience

Chapter 16

Being

*T*his section will outline step by step the best way to get the most out of this experience of The Chocolate Fast. The Fast has been created in a way so as to honor both the health aspects of fasting guidelines and the ritual elements respecting the movement of the energy within such an experience.

You are encouraged to read through the Fast first in its entirety to get a general idea of how to approach this adventure. It is recommended to follow the outline as closely as possible so as to receive the most from of the experience. Feel free to refer back to this section as often as needed; or, if you are already comfortable with the general idea of the fast—jump in and create your own magical day!

When choosing your chocolate for The Chocolate Fast, the main concept to remember is Intention. Yes, that's right, your intention is the most important thing about this fast. What is in your chocolate bar is not as momentous as what is in your mind. We've all heard the expression, 'The road to hell is paved with good intentions.' Not so! I would restate this as 'The road to hell is paved with NO intention!' Instead, living life with intention (without becoming rigid) actually brings us into alignment, the opposite of a personal 'hell'. This is one of those times to get out the heavy mental machinery. The attitude with which you approach this fast is far more determinative of your results than the particular quality of chocolate you choose to use. (Though it is always a plus to use high quality ingredients—see index for recommendations.) That said, I suggest that your chocolate selection be one you will enjoy immensely!

Remember: while chocolate does comes with inherent benefits, the more you infuse your choice of treat with your own added ingredient of appreciation, enjoyment and pleasure, the better your experience with it will be.

THE CHOCOLATE FAST

GATHER SUPPLIES:

Chocolate—Your favorite: Approximately 1-2 bars or 8-15 pieces (or the equivalent). Feel free to vary the texture and style of your chocolate delight.

Water—Pure Spring Water, 1 gallon or more.

Herbal tea (optional)—If added should, again, be high quality and organically grown.

(I recommend peppermint, jasmine, orange blossom, and lemon verbena.)

Gratitude Journal or Notebook—For recording the experience.

PREPARATION

Set aside 24-36 hours when you are not working and can give yourself your full attention. It is important that you create an atmosphere of 'self-pampering.' If possible, go to the ocean, the mountains, a lake, or some other beautiful location where you can be delighted by your scenery and not distracted by a 'messy house.' I strongly suggest doing this cleanse alone, if you can, or with another chocolate faster or supportive person. It is often easier to keep your mind set on its intention when you are alone, so if you are going to be around others, make sure you can feel completely guilt-free and fully supported, or that you are able to hold to your own course without difficulty during your fast. When questioned—or even criticized—about your 'chocolate fast,' it is important to that you be able stay in the attitude of self-care, self-love and Bliss.

CENTERING

Start the day by sitting down with a piece of chocolate on a dish and a glass of water. Begin centering yourself by taking a few deep breaths. As you exhale, release all judgment from yourself and others regarding chocolate. As you inhale, take in the idea of embracing Bliss as your natural state. Let the chocolate represent the remembrance of this state.

PARTAKING

When you feel yourself ready, open your eyes and drink down your glass of water as a symbol of cleansing the body, preparing to begin to receive this Bliss. Eat your first piece of chocolate, enjoying the taste, the texture, every part of it. With each successive bit of chocolate, see if you can experience more of the chocolate. Bring in each sense organ – smell, sound, sight along with the feel and taste of the chocolate in your mouth.

GRATITUDE

Sit with the piece of chocolate that you have consumed. Take out your gratitude journal and record the feelings you are having, and include all that you are grateful for in this moment. Let yourself continue to feel the effects and the memory of the chocolate.

Take note of your state of consciousness. If you are experiencing any negative thoughts or fears, acknowledge their presence, thank them for their presence, and notice them as if they are on their way out. You may wish to write them down. Then, let them go. Return to thoughts of gratitude.

Feel yourself at one with your decision to eat only chocolate today. Feel it as a gift you have given to yourself, and receive it gratefully.

EXPERIENCING

Continue on your day's journey, eating chocolate whenever you feel hunger or the need to snack. Enjoy it completely, and think of nothing else. Try to follow the centering, partaking, and gratitude rituals described above, even if only in abbreviated form, as they will encourage you to bring your mind back to the intention of this fast (and keep you from just downing your chocolate like bonbons on a Friday night!)

Drink water often, complemented with herbal teas as desired.

Relax, write, paint, study nature, sing, laugh, do what makes you happy!

Each time you come to another piece of chocolate, treat it like the next stage in the deeper discovery of your inner Blissful state, the one you have long been keeping yourself from discovering.

Rest as necessary. Dance as moved.

Do not be surprised if you feel new levels of joy arising in your being and you feel like dancing, singing and creating like never before.

Do not be surprised, if, on the other hand, you feel like resting and dreaming your day away. Take it as it comes. It is most important not to cast any judgment on yourself this day. It is a day of absolute pleasure and the joy of chocolate.

If you are around family and still engaged in the preparation of other meals for members of your family, honor that role while continuing to cultivate your own inner joy.

Be playful.

BECOMING

You have the opportunity this day to touch on the discovery of your natural state of inner Bliss. If you feel the awareness of this state arising, honor it with open arms and a sense of humor. Journal about: new sensations, questions, emotions, ideas, anything.

SHIFTING

You may experience what are known as 'shifts' in your energy and vibration. These can be sometimes subtle in their nature, and sometimes not so subtle. As you surrender to this experience and allow yourself to really enjoy and delight in chocolate and your time with yourself, you are removing blocks in your being on many levels, the removal of which may feel somewhat uncomfortable from time to time. Possible sensations resulting from the fast are: a feeling of spaceyness, shaking (mild to intense), headache, mild anxiety or feeling 'off,' increased energy and creativity, extreme emotions (laughter, tears), etc. These are symptoms of expansion as your energy body actually expands to take in more awareness of space. Just relax, drink more water or tea and, if possible, soak in a bath.

FLYING – THE BLISS EXPERIENCE

It is possible that you will slip into the state of Bliss, which some have compared to flying or floating. Everyone experiences this state differently. I can only say that when you are there, you know it. Enjoy it while it lasts, and don't worry about getting there. You are less likely to reach it if you are trying. Allow yourself to enjoy. To some, this state comes so naturally, it may not even seem out of the ordinary, and instead feels incredibly familiar. While to others, it may feel like a more pronounced altered state of awareness and consciousness. People are beginning to return to this state of awareness more and more these days, but it may be completely foreign to you. No biggie. Be Happy. Really. And congratulations!

If you don't find yourself there the first time, don't worry. Everyone is at a different place in their unfolding. That doesn't mean you are any less capable of reaching this state; some of us just have more cleansing, relaxing or letting go to do. Hopefully, the experience you do have will help to enlighten you as to where you need to focus your attention in order to move forward on your path.

ENDING THE FAST:

RETURNING AWARENESS TO SURROUNDINGS
(Either the next morning or after noontime the following day)
As it becomes time to bring your fast to a close, take a few moments to become aware of your surroundings, your physical body and your breath. Reconnect with the intention you had for the fast. Take care to end your fast with gratitude and thanksgiving. Rejoice in the ability to have the choice to eat chocolate all day long! It is a glorious opportunity. One you might take again soon, if you feel the call.

You may want to spend some time in quiet rest to allow your body and spirit to integrate the new awareness you have gained, and the changes in your body.

End your fast with something simple and nutritious, such as brown rice with hazelnuts and sprouts, steamed vegetables and whole grain bread. Bring in the proteins gently and let the carbs take the lead! You may instead choose to come off of your fast onto only raw foods.

Consider your regular diet and what might be most beneficial to you! Whatever you choose, be gentle with yourself.

REMEMBERING

As you move back into your normal routine, give yourself little reminders to help sustain the memory of the states of Bliss and the awareness you achieved during your Fast. Maybe you might want to continue your journaling or some other crafts or hobbies, or post pictures or writing excerpts from your fast on your favorite social networking site—anything that helps you to return mentally to your fast.

The more often you visit this space of Bliss—whether with chocolate or another pleasure you surrender to—the easier it is to keep this new state of awareness, and the more prolonged are its effects. The goal is one day to live always in this natural state of Blissful peace.

POSSIBLE CLEANSING EFFECTS

As with any form of fasting, your body food load has been greatly reduced for 24 hours and has had a chance to throw off some stored toxins. You might feel some of these effects as body aches, headache, or other mild flu-like symptoms. If this is the case, your body is signaling you that another cleanse might be in order for you. Stay on whole grains like brown rice and millet, and keep to steamed vegetables and fresh fruit drinks for several days to ease yourself back into a regular diet. (To find another more intensive cleansing program that is right for you, contact a practitioner from the list in the index.)

35. Wheel of Self-Belief

Angel Sigil

SHAMBELEK

Part 6

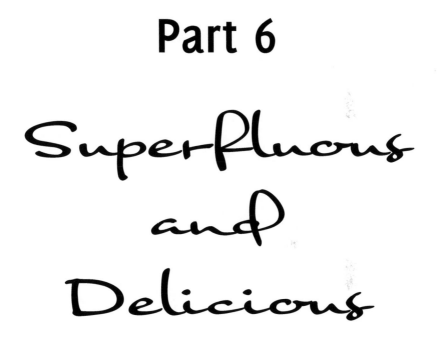

Superfluous
and
Delicious

Chapter 17

Chocolate Chakras

You can read any number of books to find out about the energy centers in the body known as chakras, (though there are new findings of the discovery of some additional chakras perhaps not as well known in times past). I will only briefly touch on them and roughly how they operate (more recent information is only now beginning to be understood).

Just like the nervous system in the body, there is a subtle energy system composed of what are called nadis (rivers). There are over 72,000 nadis in the body, and just as the nerves bundle together at certain points called a plexus, the nadis meet at distributing centers as well, known as chakras. In ancient times yogic sages experienced and recorded the knowledge of 7 main chakras, recently we have uncovered at least an additional 3 (see Almine in index) so there are a minimum of 10 main chakras in the body, which are located along the region of the spinal cord. I will discuss only the seven with which I have more intimate knowledge. If you wish to know more about the others mentioned, see the index for references. [Note: there are hundreds of thousands of chakras all over the body which distribute energy further, the ones mentioned are something like the 'control centers' for the other smaller chakras]

The original first chakra is located at the perineum (in males) and just outside the cervix (in females), the second - in the pelvic region, third - at the navel, fourth at the heart, fifth—the throat, sixth at the forehead center, and the seventh at the crown of the head. [Author's note: Additional chakras have been found two inches below the base of the spine as well as hovering over the top of the head (like the halos depicted in earlier Christian paintings). There is also a chakra in the solar plexus region]. Each chakra has a purpose in the body. Besides distributing life force energy, each center controls and is responsible for a specific level of consciousness or awareness. As consciousness expands, each successive chakra is activated and is said to have 'awakened.' Chakras can be working (i.e. spinning, distributing life force energy) without being awakened (i.e. responsible for different types of awareness). In fact, if they weren't spinning and distributing energy, the body would die. Chocolate, with its many properties and effects, resonates with nearly every chakra, as can be seen below.

Chakras and their resonance with the properties of Chocolate

Moolandhara (root): *Security, Abundance, Nourish- ment, Grounding*

Chocolate imparts to us a sense of security, the richness of abundance, the fulfillment of good nourishment on many levels and is grounding in that it is food, very physical and brown—the color of the earth. Some say raw cacao carries the vibration of prosperity and is the reason why chocolate beans made the perfect currency, one that could not be hoarded.

Swadhistana (pelvis): *Desire, Pleasure, Joy, Ecstasy, Fulfillment, Sexuality*

Chocolate has long been associated with pleasure, desire, joy and ecstasy. It is known as an aphrodisiac, and contains the 'love hormone' phenylephylamine.

When experiencing any of these emotions whilst partaking of chocolate – you are stimulating this center.

Manipura (navel): *Drive, Will, Power, Confidence, Creativity, Digestion*

People—especially women—will go to great lengths to secure their chocolate supply. It is a motivator of sorts, imbuing those who partake of it with confidence, creativity, power and drive through its ability to relax you and make you like a child again, and through its antioxidant and other health benefits. Also being food, chocolate cannot help but stimulate the center responsible for digestion and assimilation. When we consume chocolate with motivation and confidence we not only activate the digestive fires, but the spiritual fire of our being known as 'bhuta agni'.

Anahata (solar plexus): *Love, Acceptance, Embrace, Healing, Balance, Creation*

Chocolate is for the beloved, a symbol of the heart. It creates within us the same feeling we experience when in love, and is found to be healing just in the sharing of it. It is easy both to offer and accept chocolate – both emotions trigger the subtle Anahata chakra of the heart.

By giving ourselves the gift of chocolate we are activating the principles of self-love and further stimulating the beautiful energy of this chakra. By loving ourselves and sharing the gift of chocolate with ourselves and others we are creating an expansion in the frequency of the heart which, by in turn, sends out waves of healing to the planet!

Vishuddhi (throat): *Truth, Communication, Self-expression*

Chocolate is swallowed down the throat—right through this center. As one of the most desired sweets of life and a popular way to expresses love and appreciation of the heart, this center is stimulated by both the giver and receiver.

Speak your truth! If you love chocolate, speak it! By eating something you love you allow yourself to open up in this center and align with what else is your truth. This is the center which is also the gateway to experiencing the sweetness of life. Open your mouth, open your throat chakra to receive the sweet ambrosia of experiences that life has to offer!

Anja (third eye): *Intuition, Higher mind, Wisdom, Consciousness*

Chocolate (especially raw chocolate) nourishes the intellect with its wide array of nutrients. Chocolate has been the source of many works of inspiration, and when consumed mindfully can actually stimulate this center and bring the pineal gland into a state of higher function.

By opening up to the potential inherent in chocolate, we are opening to our own potential as well. Allow the delight of chocolate to inspire you, to stimulate within the connection with a deeper aspect of Self. This is the center which allows us to move beyond duality and separation-consciousness and realize that we are all connected.

Sahasara (crown): *Connection to Divine, Higher Self, Bliss*

Chocolate is thought to have come from divine origins and stimulates connection to an expanded state of awareness by prolonging the presence of the Bliss hormone anandamide in the body. What more can be said? Chocolate is one of the keys to unlocking the mysteries of Bliss! Chocolate is Bliss in physical form and by ingesting it we allow ourselves to take a step in the direction of opening to the possibilities inherent in this chakra and beyond!

> [It has been my recent experience in meditation that our lowest two energies centers have switched places. This brings us into a relationship with the world and ourselves that is based on sensuality, beauty, joy and art rather than the old paradigm of safety and security. For it is in our connectivity with all of life that we open ourselves to the free flow of abundance available to us all.]

·

Chapter 18

Chocolate Revelations

MY STORY—RAW

*T*here is a reason this chapter is last, and that is so this fast could be experienced by everyone with out any restriction on access to particular forms of chocolate. I have had my own miraculous chocolate transformations while writing this book.

The idea for this book began with the first chocolate fast I did some years ago for no particular reason whatsoever other than I had this bag of amazing chocolates and I just made a spur of the moment decision based on my naturally rebellious nature to eat only chocolate for a day. Actually, for me it was more like 36-48 hours. I basically went until I felt done—not 'sick of chocolate,' mind you, but rather finished with my experiment, and pleasantly so.

Here's that story:

My first chocolate fast began one morning in the winter of 2003. What happened, superficially, is this: all day I drank water and ate chocolate. It wasn't like I was eating it non-stop; whenever I felt hungry, instead of grabbing a sandwich or other food, I got another beautiful piece of chocolate and sat down with it like it was the only piece I had, and ate it lovingly. Every bite was delightful, and I felt fantastic! Never did I feel ill or anything less than completely healthy during the entire day.

Beneath the purely physical—and wonderful!—process, something more was going on. Each time I ate another piece of chocolate, it was like I was discovering another layer of acceptance for myself. It was obvious to me at a certain point that I had passed an invisible barrier, one that I had set up where the 'appropriate amount' of chocolate pleasure existed. I'd never known such a barrier existed in me. I had a burst of intuition then that I was touching on something beyond just my own limitations that day. I felt there was a collective restraint, one that belonged to all of society. I was (again), as at so many times before in my life, dancing with a taboo. On that day of fasting with chocolate, in those deliciously revealing moments, a realization was taking form. I realized that we all had these ideas, these self-imposed limitations regarding our ability and our right to feel joy, to feel Bliss. It occurred to me that by unveiling this secret self-denial and allowing myself to feel joy, I was helping all of humankind to do the same. We are all connected at the deepest levels, and the expansion of consciousness in just a single one of us sends waves of possibility out to us all…

And so it happened that nearly six years later I was planning to write book about self-healing that I'd been contemplating for a long time. I was attending a book-writing seminar for this purpose, when I had the realization that *The Chocolate Fast* was the book that needed to be written first. I had always joked about writing it, but deep down I was serious about the idea, and knew that one day I would.

Throughout the writing process, and all the research and reading, I was all the while seeking inspiration from chocolate itself, sampling nearly every form of it I could find. My son of age 16 months at the time was really beginning to be interested in all foods, and I felt a little wrong about eating something in front of him that I wouldn't give him or was at all uncomfortable with him putting in his developing young body and mind. (I began to question that whole reasoning process). I started to buy the 'healthiest' versions of chocolate I could find. (There are some good ones out there). I wasn't very familiar with raw chocolate at the time, but in my research I began to delve into it, and examined all its supposed health benefits. I did a little more research and hunted down some local distributors of such treats. I was not sold right away; the flavor of raw, unprocessed chocolate was different from what I was used to, and the texture was a bit of a change, as well.

It was around this point that I came across David Wolfe's book Naked Chocolate, which is all about raw chocolate. In his book, David gives a few simple recipes for making raw chocolates. I began to experiment with these, feeding the results to my son, as well. I was thrilled at the prospect of being able to eat chocolate with my son without the dual concerns of sugar (the recipes in the book called for agave nectar) and caffeine (raw chocolate has almost none). Plus, after reading the amazing list of nutrients found in pre-processed cacao (see a portion in index) I was totally won over.

And this is where my journey as a *chocolatier* began.

Since starting work on this book, I have created a raw chocolate business with one of my girlfriends. It has been enormously exciting to integrate so much of my other healing wisdom into these unique confections of transformation. We use only the finest ingredients and the purest of intent.

So, of course when I do the chocolate fast (which is every week now) I do it using raw chocolate and I feel an added element of support in the journey from the amazing nutrients available in raw ingredients.

Check out the web and keep your eye open for future publications to tell you more about Raw Transformational chocolates and other tools for transformation, if you are so inclined.

OTHER STORIES

Here is a story I found during my research on chocolate that really inspired me. The example of this "chocoholic" epitomizes the point I am making with this book.

A petite Midland mother who claims she has survived on almost nothing but chocolate for 49 years says the sweet stuff has kept her as fit and healthy as a teenager.

Chocoholic Cathy Creegan, who works as a library assistant at Solihull College, says she never eats a normal meal, opting instead for bars of chocolate.

The seven-and-a-half stone mother-of-two confessed to spending up to 200 pounds a month on chocolate and admitted she had already eaten 15 Easter eggs.

Mrs Creegan said: "I love everything about chocolate. The look of it, the sound of it when I unwrap it, the feel of it melting in my mouth and obviously the taste of it.

"It's the way I live my life. I'm hardly ever ill. I feel like a teenager.

"The very thought of pasta, rice, beef, bacon, fish or cheese just makes me gag. It's not just the taste of it, it's the feel of it and the thought of it."

Mrs. Creegan's husband Trevor, an aircraft engineer, and her sons Stephen, aged 28, and Jessie, aged 26, have learnt never to pinch their mother's chocolate, hidden in cupboards and tins all over the house.

She said: "I buy big boxes of it from the cash and carry, and the sight of bar after bar of perfect chocolate makes me so excited. Then I take all the bars out of the box and I put them in my secret hiding places.

"I get so angry if anyone eats my chocolate. I always know if my husband has been near my chocolate because he leaves the cupboards open. He knows now that if he eats my chocolate he has to buy me some to replace it. I know it sounds mean, but chocolate is my staple.

"The only other thing I eat apart from chocolate is potato. I can manage the odd bowl of mash or a couple of roast potatoes. I've always been like this, ever since I was a baby. My parents thought I would grow out of it, but I never did."

Mr. Creegan said: "The rest of the family eats well. Whenever we go to a friend's house for dinner, they just cook her a bowl of mash and give her some chocolate. No-one minds - it's just the way she is."

By Jessica Shepherd, Birmingham Post

DAVID'S STORY:

Until about three years ago, my idea of a fast was limited to my experience of being raised under the dubious auspices of the Roman Catholic church: during the Lenten season, we were to eat no meat—except fish, of course—on Fridays, and no snacks between meals. That any of us considered that this amounted to some kind of sacrifice—and it did, incredibly, to most of us— is testament to the habit of wanton consumption that has for too long characterized the American way of life, our particular religious affiliations not excepted. Of those individuals who would willingly abstain from eating for more than a few hours at a time, I was aware of two classes: sufferers of eating disorders, and wrestlers trying to make weight for an approaching contest— neither of whom had as their end a goal that could be called spiritual in the usual sense of the word, or a concern for health as we generally understand it.

After some years of dabbling in the world of yoga, I became exposed to the notion that fasting could be something much more than what I had previously assumed it to be. First, I was led to understand that enormous health benefits accrued to specific forms of fasting, some more than others. Second, I learned that a fast could not only clean one out physically, it could also effect a spiritual purification as well. This seems glaringly obvious to me now, of course; raised as I was, the stories of Jesus' fast and his temptation, and of all the "desert saints," could not have escaped me. But in the end they only served, thanks to my general disenchantment with the faith of my forebears, to prejudice me where the subject of fasting was concerned.

Never one to do anything half-heartedly, I decided to jump right into the business with what is now commonly referred to as the "lemonade fast." (Nothing but the juice and pulp of organically grown lemons, mixed with cayenne pepper and Grade B maple syrup.) I stuck with it the recommended 10 days (although it is suggested that one go beyond this to achieve the maximum physical cleansing or detoxification). It was an extraordinary experience, and on both the physical and spiritual fronts I reaped enormous benefits. Ultimately, however, it left me with a bad taste in my mouth. For one thing, at the end of the ordeal I was so ravenous for the taste of "real food" that I found it impossible to ease back into my usual diet, and suffered a good bit of gastro-intestinal distress as a result. (I've found that this is a common difficulty when coming off an intensive fast of this nature.)

More importantly, I questioned why such a huge commitment and sacrifice should be required to get more spiritually "in touch" with one's Self and with Life. I could understand the necessity in terms of the aim of physical detoxification, certainly. But my physical health and dietary habits having been pretty good to begin with, I was much more interested in effecting changes within me on the spiritual level.

Are such extreme measures really demanded for the attainment of a feeling of deeper spiritual connection in this life? Do we need to go so very far to get back into tune with our true place and relationship in the universe?

When Stasia told me about her Chocolate Fast, I was skeptical, of course. What value could there possibly be in eating nothing but chocolate for a day—other than the obvious "naughty" gastronomic pleasure of doing so? She assured me I would be pleasantly surprised, and that I would get much more out of it than I expected to. I decided, Sure, what have I got to lose? (She didn't need to twist my arm much, as you can guess; and it's not like I needed to psych myself up…we're talking about chocolate, after all!)

As it turned out, I was more than pleasantly surprised. I followed the guidelines for the fast as Stasia lays them out in her book, and although I wasn't able to devote a whole day to myself in the way she prescribes—I had a lot of work to get done that day—it really didn't seem to matter. Whenever I felt hungry, I sat down with my two or three organic raw truffles, and I felt I was entering into a sacred meditative space. I came out of it every time feeling more spiritually focused, more centered, more in tune with the moment than I had been before the ritual. Throughout the day I became aware that I was experiencing a greater and more refined sensitivity to life, and deeper feeling of connection with Spirit (or God, or Life—however you choose to denominate It) and with my fellow human beings.

Unlike my other fasting experiences, I never felt that I was denying myself anything. No "will power" needed to be exercised. It was a piece of cake (almost literally!), and gratifying on so many levels, I can't wait to do it again! I wonder if, based on the quite incredible nutritional content of raw cacao, it's not the best fasting option in existence. I look forward to many more—and longer—chocolate fasts in the future, to give my body a much-needed break and my spirit a welcome boost. Thank you, Stasia Bliss, for opening my eyes, heart, and mouth to the gift of raw chocolate, and The Chocolate Fast.

TERRA'S STORY:

On first impulse, I was REALLY excited about doing the Chocolate Fast. I have done many fasts, one as long as ten days. I know what it feels like to clear my body and mind of all food and preparation and thinking about my next meal, and so on. I love the way I feel when a fast is complete: so clear and open... And to do a fast where the only thing I take in is chocolate (and water)... WOW!! REALLY? OK!

I have been allergic to caffeine since I was 16 when something clicked in my body (the same thing also happened to my mom when she turned 16 and my brother when he turned 16). Too much caffeine in any form would cause joint stiffness, headaches, muscle tightness, and eventually a blinding migraine. So by age 19, I had figured out how to (mostly) live without chocolate, Dr. Pepper, and sweet tea (and I am from the South!! Not an easy task!) If I chose to have anything with caffeine in it, it was always chocolate and in very limited amounts.

And then, about two years ago, I found out about raw chocolate!!! I can eat as much raw chocolate as I want with no negative side effects! I have tested the theory many times and with many different raw chocolate products. It has been a fun and exciting adventure and I feel like a kid let loose in, well, a candy shop! I decided to do more research on the Chocolate Fast. I GET TO eat as much chocolate as I want, and ONLY chocolate, for a whole day! Let's go!

So, I started my day with a raw chocolate smoothie. That got me through several hours. I drank water through the morning, and then, I had some raw chocolate truffles I had made with my friend. WOW! We got to put some yummy energy into the chocolates to support my cleansing process, and I had LOTS of awesome chocolate to unite with through the day. We also made some Chocolate Super Butter[TM?]. We put some of the butter into the truffles and I was able to use the butter as another chocolate staple to eat through the day.

By the time I was halfway through the day, I started noticing some of the effects of doing a fast... The first few hours of the first day of a fast can sometimes be a challenge. Your body starts cleansing and letting go of toxins. This started right away. I was a little frustrated at first because I wanted to enjoy the chocolate! And then, I realized I was letting go of some of the old toxic beliefs as well as some of the physical toxins in my body. I had to let go of the belief that I am "allergic" to chocolate! I had to let go of the belief that chocolate is BAD! It was never the chocolate! It was the way the chocolate was processed, plus all the other stuff that goes into the chocolate. Now, for me, that was important. Many people do not react to chocolate the same way I have throughout my life. Heated chocolate does not have the same effect on everyone as it did on me, but it was a huge revelation for me to let go of the thought that chocolate is bad for me. I was so happy to let that one go!

As for the rest of the day, I continued cleansing, I continued enjoying my chocolate, and I continued looking forward to my next love affair with the next truffle or bite of chocolate super butter. It was true Bliss. I was so glad I got the chance to try this fast and I am so happy to share my experience with more people. I hope you have just as awesome an experience of awareness, openness, and expansion when you do your fast. To Bliss!!! Bliss.

~Terra Bundance September, 2009

IAM BLOOM'S STORY:

When I heard of the chocolate fast, I was more than a little interested. I am a chocolate fiend. I have to have chocolate at some point in the day, it really is a necessity, so I was excited to see what would happen.

Before this fast my exposure to raw chocolate was very limited, but I had the wonderful opportunity to fast with intentional raw chocolate made by Stasia and myself. After eating nothing but raw chocolate all day, I highly recommend raw chocolate for any real chocolate lover (especially if you hadn't had the chance to have it), I have to say that there is nothing in the world that compares to how you feel eating it.

I followed the fast just as it is laid out here. I drank water (in fact I had a craving for water and went from drinking a liter in a day to 3 or 4) and ate chocolate when I got hungry, simple. The fast itself was awesome, but I didn't notice anything that stood out to me until the next day. The next time I do the fast I think I will include some nice organic teas to it and make sure I have time to do nothing but reflect. As it was, I had to work that day so I wasn't completely focused as I would like to be next time.

I had been wanting to modify my diet before the fast, but hadn't really been able to put it into practice. Basically I wanted to cut out all meat from my diet and just eat when my body was actually hungry (as opposed to eating 'three square meals' a day, which I knew was more than I needed). The fast gave me the push I needed to really dive into my new eating habits.

After having an absolutely satisfying day of eating chocolate, I found that my body had kind of reset... as had my mental/ emotional cravings for food. I wasn't hungry for anything that I had wanted before, like meat, cheese, and generally over processed foods. I also found that I was only hungry and started taking in calories that my body needed in relation to my routine. When I am not exercising or exerting myself I find I only need one meal and one snack during the day, more depending on the level of activity.

I felt so clean and joyful after my fast and it has carried me through the last month for sure. Thank you Stasia and all your wonderfully magical ideas! Just try one day, I guarantee that you will want to repeat the fast.

GENESIS DIONNE'S STORY:

I was greatly surprised by how much fun and peace I gained access to through the chocolate fasting workshop that I attended with Stasia and Terra last spring.

I had no idea what to expect going into the experience but I was quickly made comfortable and was moved by how open the people that attended were. As we moved through the chocolate tasting and the exercises that supported the "flavor" of the chocolate I gained access to really indulging in life and the flavor of intentions.

The intentions of the chocolate flavors opened me up to what intentions I place in my everyday activities and food. I gained greater perspective to the importance of indulging and how putting proper intention into any experience can lead to great satisfaction and peace of mind.

I often refer friends to Stasia's book and concept of indulging or fasting with intention and am grateful for the experience and what it has opened up for me in my own life.

CLOSING –

The experience of this journey has been multi-dimensional. By that I mean that you have been given information on more than one level of your being. You will continue to notice the effects of this practice long after you put down this book, long after you do the fast.

The meditations throughout this book have been a form of yoga Nidra, an ancient yogic practice to bring you into deeper conscious awareness of the many levels of your being. If you feel called, read the meditations again and again, with or without the chapters. Their simplicity will have profound change on your life.

I would like to complete this journey with you by expressing my deep gratitude. It has been an experience of joy and Bliss to travel this path with you. It is my sincere hope and wish for you that you find the Bliss that awaits you – inside!

From this day forward I challenge you to allow chocolate, and all else that you encounter, to be a gateway into alignment. To use every seeming obstacle and every pleasure as an opportunity to embrace the moment and to find Bliss as the present's gift.

Much love to you my family!

Chocolate Recommendations

Many times throughout this book I mention French chocolate specialist Chloe Doutre-Roussel, whom I met while reading the charming tale <u>Chocolate: The Bittersweet Saga of Dark and Light</u> by Mort Rosenblum. Her basic philosophy is simple:

> *"Forget the meaningless catch-all word chocolate and find out what sorts of chocolate speak to your soul and body. Everyone's personal 'package' is unique. Once you know what you're after, the rewards are beyond measure."*

In chocolate, I have my personal favorites, as I am sure you do. The most important part about *The Chocolate Fast* is choosing the chocolate that most delights you, for it is the experience, the intention and the feelings you are able to conjure that will make it most beneficial to you, beyond the chocolate's actual nutritional value. But if you are like me, you have the added element of the healthiest and most "intentional" chocolate on the planet I include here a few of my favorites and why I think they are superb selections for The Chocolate Fast.

Never the Same Chocolate: Always Amazing, Never the Same! ~ My own chocolate! This chocolate is made with intention, therapeutic food-grade essential oils and my partner in chocolate & best friend -Terra Bundance. This chocolate is transformational food. I guarantee there is nothing else like it on the planet! All raw, all vegan, gluten-free and sweetened with raw coconut nectar, agave and yacon—delicious! Not to mention the use of very intentional 'consciousness elements' (ask us more about this)! We create unique and specialized chocolate just for you, to support your current phase of transformation…contact us today!

www.neverthesamechocolate.com

www.journeyonpurpose.org

Health By Chocolate ~ A company has embraced the intentional aspect of creating chocolates that are a healthy addition to your life. Just the name alone is enough to put it up on my list of choices. Website: www.healthbychocolate.com

LuLu's Raw Chocolate Alchemy ~ Local Portland, Oregon artist LuLu has created both raw chocolate bars and raw chocolate spreads that are delightful. A great choice for anyone wanting to 'go raw' and enjoy the full spectrum of benefits that chocolate has to offer. Website: www.luluschocolate.com

Intentional Chocolate ~ Here is a company that has put intention to work for them in the highest capacity. They actually have monks chanting over their chocolate to make theirs of the highest vibrational quality. They have gone so far as to do studies on people before and after consuming their chocolate to demonstrate the benefits of so exceptional ingredient as a healthy dose of intent. Website: www.intentionalchocolate.com

Raw Chocolate by Sunfoods.com ~ This site is owned by David Wolfe who is the author of several books including the wonderful book on raw chocolate, _Naked Chocolate_. He has a number of products to make your own as well as some chocolate bars using only the finest raw ingredients.

Gnosis Chocolate ~ This magical raw chocolate is made by chocolate girl Vanessa—out of New York City and absolutely divine! She puts all kinds of superfoods, herbs, intention and love into her chocolate. Another favorite of mine! Website: www.gnosischocolate.com

As you have probably noticed, most of my recommendations are raw chocolate purveyors. You can do the fast with any chocolate of your choosing, of course, but as long as I am making recommendations, raw chocolate is the chocolate of chocolates.

Raw chocolate, also known as Cacao, is a true superfood unlike anything before! The ancient Aztec, Maya, and Olmec were really onto something!

Health Benefits/Nutritional Profile

The truth is, chocolate is very, very good for you. Honestly. Chocolate in its raw form contains a long list of key nutrients qualifying it as a 'superfood.' Chocolate greatest benefits are delivered when taken in its natural form, the cacao bean, or the broken version of the bean called 'nibs.'

Raw Cacao is the highest known source of anti-oxidants by a factor of almost 5! It has nearly 20 times the antioxidant levels of red wine and up to 30 times what is found in green tea!* A new laboratory test known as ORAC (Oxygen Radical Absorbance Capacity) was developed by USDA researchers at Tufts University to rate the antioxidant levels of fruits and vegetables. Here are the results of raw organic cacao:

Montezuma drank the chocolate bean in small amounts up to fifty times a day for increased virility; Aztecs believed that wisdom and power came from eating the fruit of the Cacao tree. They also believed it to be nourishing and fortifying, in addition to being a powerful aphrodisiac. Still today chocolate is given at Valentine's Day in hopes of tapping this historically renowned quality.

Cacao beans contain no sugar and between 12% and 50% fat depending on variety and growth conditions. There is no evidence to implicate cacao bean consumption with obesity.

Cacao is remarkably rich in magnesium; it appears to be the #1 source of magnesium of any food. This is likely the primary reason women crave chocolate during the menstrual period. Magnesium balances brain chemistry, builds strong bones, and is associated with more happiness. Magnesium is the most deficient major mineral on the Standard American Diet (SAD); over 80% of Americans are chronically deficient in magnesium!

Cacao does contain trace amounts of caffeine and theobromine. However, experiments have shown that these stimulants are far different when the bean is consumed raw as opposed to roasted. Like everywhere else, raw is better.

Consider the following: Experimental research of chocolate by homeopaths indicates its stimulating effect when cooked. One experiment conducted with a decoction of roasted ground cacao beans in boiling water produced an excitement of the nervous system similar to that caused by black coffee, an excited state of circulation, and an accelerated pulse. Interestingly, when the same decoction was made with raw, unroasted beans neither effect was noticeable, leading the researchers to conclude that the physiological changes were caused by aromatic substances released during roasting.

Cacao seems to diminish appetite, probably due to its monoamine oxidase enzyme inhibitors (MAO inhibitors). These digestive enzyme inhibitors differ from those found in most nuts and seeds. These rare MAO inhibitors actually produce favorable results when consumed by allowing more serotonin and other neurotransmitters to circulate in the brain. According to Dr. Gabriel Cousens, MAO inhibitors facilitate youthening and rejuvenation.

Phenyl ethylamine (PEA) is also found in chocolate. PEA is an adrenal-related chemical that is also created within the brain and released when we are in love. This is one of the reasons why love and chocolate have such a longstanding correlation. PEA also plays a role in increasing focus and alertness.

Concerning allergies, it is important to note that a recent study showed that only one out of 500 people who thought they were allergic to chocolate actually tested positive. Allergies to chocolate are quite rare. It is typically the case that the person is in fact allergic to milk and dairy products.

(http://www.thepowermall.com/thecenterforhealth/healthy_food/chocolate.htm)

Cacao is high in the beauty mineral sulfur. Sulfur builds strong nails, hair and shiny skin, detoxifies the liver, and supports healthy pancreas functioning. Anecdotal reports indicate that cacao is so high in sulfur it detoxifies mercury.

(http://www.alivefoods.com/cacao.html)

Researchers have found that raw and/or minimally processed cocoa contains flavanoids similar to those found in green tea. According to preliminary studies, these antioxidants have been linked to helping accomplish the following:

Decrease blood pressure
Improve circulation
Lower death rate from heart disease
Improve function of endothelial cells that line the blood vessels
Defend against destructive molecules called free radicals, which trigger cancer, heart disease and stroke
Improve digestion and stimulate kidneys
Help treat patients with anemia, kidney stones and poor appetite

Though raw cacao is best for receiving maximum benefits and the greatest quantity of nutrients, chocolate in its most familiar form has received praise for heart health, lowering cholesterol and delivering antioxidants.

So with all of these remarkable health benefits, where did we get the notion that chocolate wasn't good for us? Well, most of the health problems are generally linked to the addition of other ingredients to chocolate such as milk, sugar and preservatives. And as mentioned, the raw form of chocolate is the most beneficial, containing the most nutrients and the least harmful side effects.

When looking for chocolate to tickle your sweet tooth, the least harmful sweetener to consume with the cacao bean is agave nectar. Agave nectar comes right from the agave cactus (the same one used to make tequila). Agave has a very low rating on the glycemic index, which means that it does not make your blood sugar spike when consumed, and is safe for diabetics.

In the index I've included some additional information about agave and other sweet alternatives to sugar. So what's the gripe with sugar other than making you fat? Well, for one thing it suppresses the immune functions of the body for up to 8 hours after its consumption. Hmmm?

Here's a brief glimpse at Cacao's Nutritional Facts from <u>Naked Chocolate</u>:

CALCIUM 800 - 1,100 ppm
CARBOHYDRATES 347,000 - 445,000 ppm
CHROMIUM (highest of any major food)
COPPER 24 ppm
DOPAMINE
FIBER 59,000 - 89,000 ppm
GLUTAMIC-ACID 10,200 ppm
IRON 36 - 37 ppm
LYSINE 800 ppm
MAGNESIUM
PANTOTHENIC-ACID (Vitamin B-5) 13ppm
PHENYLALANINE 5,600 ppm
PROTEIN 120,000 - 180,000 ppm
SEROTONIN**

(**Quoted from, and for a complete list of Nutrition Facts on Raw Cacao see: <u>Naked Chocolate</u> by David Wolfe & Shazzie.)

Chocolate Studies

There have been many different studies showing the possible effects of chocolate consumption on groups of participants.

One such study by the Associated Press entitled 'Study: Dark chocolate Lowers Blood Pressure' printed on August 27, 2003 which appears in the Journal of the American Medical Association included 13 adults with untreated mild hypertension. Each of them ate 3-ounce chocolate bars every day for two weeks. Half of them received white chocolate while the other half got dark chocolate. Blood pressure was shown to be relatively unchanged for those who ate the white chocolate, but the dark chocolate eaters' blood pressure showed significant changes. Their systolic blood pressure dropped an average of 5 points and their diastolic reading dropped an average of nearly two points.

In another study conducted at Pennsylvania State University by study leader Penny Kris-Etherton, a group of participants, split into two groups, ate the same low fat diet except for one of the groups got a chocolate bar and the other group received a high-carb snack. The groups later switched snacks. Total blood cholesterol and LDL ("bad") cholesterol levels didn't vary with either snack. But, increases in HDL ("good") cholesterol and reductions in triglycerides (a heart-risky type of blood fat) were found in the people eating chocolate.

However, it is important to note that these health benefits are seen for people who eat traditional chocolate bars that include minimal amounts of heavily processed cocoa that have been blended with large amounts of sugars, dairy products, and artificial flavorings. But rather, to benefit from eating chocolate, one should be eating dark chocolates that have a high percentage of cocoa content. Even more beneficial to one's health is eating cocoa is the crudest format possible.

Raw cacao or chocolate should not be confused with other substances such as coco (coconut), kola (a nut whose flavor is used in soft drinks), or coca (the leaf of the plant from which cocaine is derived). Cocoa and cocoa butter are cooked, processed substances derived from raw cacao nibs (or beans/nuts).

Over 80% of the US population is deficient in magnesium. In nature, the primary source of magnesium is cacao (raw chocolate beans)!**

Raw Cacao actually diminishes appetite and aids in weight loss…

Increases sensuality and beauty…

Helps to heal and open the heart…

Nourishes the intellect and attracts prosperity…

The flavor of raw cacao is similar to dark, bitter chocolate. It is delicious eaten alone, with agave nectar, or in your favorite smoothie! For some of the most spectacular raw cacao recipes, I recommend the recently released *Naked Chocolate*, by David Wolfe and Shazzie. One of the main differences between raw cacao and the chocolate typically available on the open market (cocoa—a processed substance) is that raw cacao has all the original healthy cacao butter, containing all the essential fatty acids and amazing taste naturally found in the bean. All chocolate starts out as raw cacao beans (or nuts—they are actually the seed of the cacao fruit which grows on a tropical tree). Processing, cooking and roasting corrupt the delicate, complex flavor of the cacao nib (the bean without the skin). Raw cacao is one of the most, if not **the** most, nutrient rich and complex foods known to man.

*NOTE: These statements have not been evaluated by the FDA. Raw Chocolate is not intended to diagnose, treat, cure or prevent any disease.

**NOTE: Information was obtained from the newly released book, Naked Chocolate by David Wolfe and Shazzie.

Recipes

AMAZING MEAL-REPLACER SMOOTHIE

3 Tbsp raw cacao nibs (soaked in 1 cup warm water)
1 Tbsp raw cacao powder
1 cup rice or soymilk or other milk substitute
1 cup peach or grape juice (or other juice)
½ cup coconut milk
1 Tbsp maca powder
1 Tbsp mesquite powder
1 Tbsp hemp protein powder
Frozen fruit (blueberries, strawberries, coconut chips, bananas, etc.)
1 Tbsp agave nectar

Soak the cacao nibs until they are as soft as you want them to be (anywhere from 5 minutes to half an hour). Place all the ingredients in a blender and blend until smooth. You can experiment with other ingredients, or leave some out according to their availability and your preference. Some great additions to this smoothie: goji berries, dates, figs, nut butters, hemp oil, coconut butter—the list goes on. Go crazy!

SIMPLE RAW FUDGE

1 cup pistachios (ground)
½ cup raw cacao powder
½ cup raw nibs (ground)
1 cup coconut butter
½ cup agave nectar
1 Tbsp maca powder

Mix together powders, add agave and coconut butter. Mix until smooth. Place approx. 1 teaspoon each slot of an ice cube tray. Freeze 10 min. & move to refrigerator. Enjoy cool. (Coconut butter will soften at room temperature.)

CHOCA-MACA POST-WORKOUT TODY

1-2 c. your favorite nut milk
1 T. Maca powder
1 T. Raw Cacao powder
Agave nectar to taste

Gently warm milk on low heat whisking in the powders until dissolved. Remove from heat before the concoction gets too warm (maintaining nutritional integrity) add agave nectar to taste. Enjoy! Maca and Raw Cacao give a much needed boost after workouts and assist in recovery time, muscle strength and glandular health. Really tasty for a treat too!

CHOCOLATE FUDGE

1/2 c. raw coconut butter
½ c. raw coconut oil (unrefined)
¼ c. raw cacao powder
1/8 c. raw agave nectar
Shredded coconut (unsweetened)
1 c. dates
½ c. hazelnut (or other nut) meal

Blend dates and hazelnut meal in food processor. Press into lightly oiled (with coconut oil) deep dish pan – I use a glass bread pan. Boil water and set aside. In a metal bowl place coconut butter & oil and dunk the bottom of the bowl into boiled water to gently melt.
Add to the coconut liquid agave and then cacao powder. Pour over nut crust. Refrigerate. Wait 15 minutes or so and sprinkle coconut shreds on top of hardening fudge. When solid – cut and enjoy!!! YUMMY

Tea Sources

The Tao of Tea – www.taooftea.com **– located in Portland, OR.** The owner and tea lord of this amazing teahouse is Veerinder Chawla. He started this company with a simple 'love of the leaf,' he says. He travels to the source to provide amazingly fresh teas cultivated with love. The Tao of Tea offers single teas and blends— many options to choose from here! So take your time in your selection. Everything he sells is of the highest quality.

Organic India – www.organicindia.com. One of my favorite vendors, they offer amazing tulsi tea blends. Tulsi, also referred to as 'holy basil,' is a principle herb in Ayurvedic medicine. Holy Basil is known as 'The Incomparable One' and 'The Queen of all Herbs.' One of my all-time favorites teas is Organic India's Rose Tulsi. Yum!

Yogi Tea – www.yogiproducts.com

Traditional Medicine teas – a delightful variety of medicinal teas – all pharmacopeial grade/food grade.

www.traditionalmedicines.com

Numi tea: www.worldpantry.com

Cleansing & Fasting Practitioners

The majority of these practitioners are based in or near Portland, Oregon. **I'm sure, in this day and age, the reader won't have too much trouble finding comparable services in our near her home base.**

Tashi Rana - Field of Greens- Raw Food chef, nutrition guide, diet/detox specialist, yoga instructor www.fieldofgreens.us

Chef BeLive – Gourmet Raw Culinary Artist www.chefbelive.com

Monica Peterson, MH—Master Herbalist, Holistic Iridologist, Nutrition Consultant. Currently Practicing in Salt Lake City, UT. Email: monica.marie79@gmail.com

Ericha Clare, ND—An avid believer in the adage, "You are what you eat," Dr. Clare considers cleansing a process we participate in every day. She enthusiastically helps patients incorporate raw and living foods into their life, and also guides juice fasting. Email: dr.eclare@gmail.com.
Website: www.simplynourishing.com

Dr. Rian Herscher, ND—Dietary counseling, homeopathy, botanical medicine, flower essence therapy & pharmacology. Treats the whole person, addressing lifestyle, diet, and natural medicines. Blue Sky Wellness Studio, 3944 N Mississippi Ave. Portland, OR.
   Email: drrian.nd@gmail.com
   Website: www.blueskyportland.com

Ossi Viljakainen (Acarya Omkarnath???)—Ayurveda health consultant, Yoga & meditation teacher.
Weblink: www.facebook.com/l/;http://www.amritsamgha.org
+48-74-8139-881 (landline)
Skype: ossiviljakainen
ossi.viljakainen@http://www.facebook.com/l/;iki.fi

Yoga Centers & Teachers who teach yogic philosophy

Bihar Yoga Bharati—Yogic lifestyle immersion courses in Bihar, India. Website: www.yogavision.net/byb/welcome.htm

Tashi Rana – Kundalini Yoga instructor/Raw food chef www.fieldofgreens.us

Rebecca Perry –Hatha Yoga Private & corporate instruction. Portland, OR. Website: www.yogatry.net

Michael Sapiro & Maitri house yoga – promotes conscious learning & living. Classes, Dharma talks, Thai cooking/Ayurvedic health. Michael was a Thai monk for some time and now lives in San Francisco with his lovely Thai wife. www.maitrihouseyoga.com

Elizabeth Bradley (E.B.) Ferdig—Yoga therapy. Portland, OR. www.ebyogatherapy.com

Shivadasi – New York ; private yoga instruction, corporate yoga, readings, etc. www.shivadasi.com

Sannyasin Yoga Mudra—Satyananda yoga teacher. *Arts du cirque et du yoga.* Lille, France. Email: yogamudrananda@gmail.com

Ossi Viljakainen (Acarya Omkarnath)—Ayurveda health consultant, yoga & meditation teacher. Weblink: www.facebook.com/l/;http://www.amritsamgha.org

+48-74-8139-881 (landline)
Skype: ossiviljakainen
ossi.viljakainen@http://www.facebook.com/l/;iki.fi

Yoga Shala—Portland, OR.; teacher training classes, workshops. www.yogashalapdx.com

Yoga Union Community Wellness Center—Portland, OR. www.yogaunioncwc.com

Ombase Yoga – Hillsdale, OR. www.ombase.org

OTHER AMAZING TEACHERS OF AWARENESS:

Terra Bundance – Portland, OR. ~ One-Life Practitioner, singer/songwriter/author www.terrabundance.com

Almine – Mystic, Seer, Author www.spiritualjourneys.com

Stephanie Besson – Norwalk, CT. ~ Transformational LMT, Shamaness – www.inner-strength.vpweb.com

Meditations

1ST CHAKRA 'OPEN-EYE' MEDITATION

Find yourself a comfortable upright, seated position. You can do this while holding the book; just relax your hands and shoulders as much as possible. If you would like, and if someone is handy, you can have another person read this part to you.

Take a deep breath in. Find that pause at the top of your breath. Now exhale completely and find that pause at the bottom. Do this a few times, attempting to release thoughts and burdens of the mind with each exhalation. You are clearing your mind.

Say to yourself mentally: 'I have a clear and open mind.' Repeat 3 times.

It is important to have an open mind in order to experience the journey through the chakras as previously discussed. If you are uncomfortable moving through the chakras in this way, feel free to skip this section and move right on to the next chapter.

Bring your awareness now to the pelvis and how it is touching down. Become aware of the pelvis as the base of your posture. Notice how this giant bone supports you in your seated position. Let your consciousness rest at the pelvic floor. This is the seat of what is known as your first chakra, called 'Moolandhara.' For a male, the actual center is situated between the scrotum and the anus; [perineum] for a woman, it is just outside the cervix. You can think of the chakra (or energy center) as sort of nerve plexus, but on a more subtle 'energy' level. In Chinese medicine, the energy is called Chi. The Chi travels along meridians or energy channels. In Yoga, the energy is known as prana, and the energy channels are called nadis (nadi = river). Each vital center (chakra) is responsible for bringing energy or life-force (prana) to different parts of the body, including organs and glands. Moolandhara is responsible for the lower limbs in the body, as well as for the organs of elimination.

With this expanded knowledge, bring your attention to the area of your first energy center. Begin to imagine breathing in through this center. Draw in breath as if from the pelvic floor. Allow yourself to feel nourished by this center as it sends new prana to the lower parts of your body. Along with nourishing your organs with prana, chakras also influence our consciousness. The more prana we take in, the higher we vibrate and the more awareness we have. This lowest center is related to our survival instincts: food, clothing, shelter. It is actually the highest chakra in animals.

Begin to feel, in this part of your being, that you have plenty. Begin to feel that you have all that you need to survive. Feel supported in this center. Experience the actual physical support once again of the floor beneath you. Begin to say 'yes' into this center. Say to yourself mentally: "Yes! I am supported. I have all that I need to survive. I am prosperous. There is plenty for me and everyone!" As you begin to allow these affirmations into your field, something happens to your Moolandhara center: it begins to awaken.

Before your first center awakens, you are influenced by the consciousness that is animal in you. Your survival instinct is active and you have concern for 'where the money is going to come from,' 'how to obtain food,' etc. After this center awakens, as it is now, you begin to become aware of the consciousness of plenty. Your awareness begins to expand to encompass the knowledge that there is more—more food, more money, more awareness than you were previously aware of. A trust begins to be ignited within you, for the 'rest' of you, the higher aspects of you, are beginning to again become known to you.

The first two energy centers, when they are asleep, hold us down and keep us struggling in this world. Once we awaken them, once we integrate their teachings and expand our awareness to the higher centers, we are free, both metaphorically and literally, to be all that we are and more!

So now, in this first center say again 'Yes! Yes! Yes!

All that I need is provided for me in the very moment I need it, and then some.'

As this idea seeps into your consciousness from the vaults of your remembrance, allow it to plant a seed, a seed that will sprout and grow into your full blooming consciousness as long as you continue to water it with awareness and intention.

Feel the weight of your pelvis again on the surface where you are seated. Notice your spine reaching upward. Take a deep breath in and exhale completely.

Rest for at least 1 minute without moving to integrate this new awareness. *Namaste.*

.

Select Bibliography

Almine. "The Mystical Union of the Gold and Silver." www. spiritualjourneys.com radio show archives, Sept. 13, 2008.

"The Twelve Bodies of Man." www.alminehealing.com/ cuttingedge9. html

Wheels/Images used with permission from www.spiritualjourneys. com & http://www.astrology-of-isis.com. Credit to Eva for self-wheels & Karen for angel sigils

Anderson, Richard, N.D., NMD. *Cleanse and Purify Thyself.* Medford: Christobe Publishing, 2007.

Braden, Gregg. *The Divine Matrix. California:* Hay House, 2007.

Emotions of Health. http://www.personal-development.com/ yasha/ emotions-health.htm

Haye, Louis. *You Can Heal your Life.* California: Hay House, 1984.

Heart Math. www.heartmath.org

Holliwell, Raymond. *Working with the Law.* Scottsdale: Life Success Productions, 2007.

Lowery, Linda. *The Chocolate Tree: A Mayan folktale.* Minneapolis: Millbrook Press, 2009.

Quan Yin, Amorah. *The Pleadian Workbook: Awakening your Divine Ka.* Rochester: Bear and Company, 1995.

Rosenblum, Mort. *Chocolate: A Bittersweet Saga of Dark and Light. San Francisco:* Northpoint Press, 2006.

Saraswati, Swami Niranjanananda. *Yoga Darshan*. Bihar: Yoga Publishing Trust, 2002.

Saraswati, Swami Satyananda. *Kundalini Tantra*. Bihar: Yoga Publishing Trust, 2001.

Wikipedia. "Liver Functions, Indulgences, Fasting."

Wolfe, David and Shazzie. *Naked Chocolate*. Sunfood Nutrition - San Diego: Maul Brothers publishing , 2005.

Thanks

I would like to thank, first and foremost, David Brown IV for his help in editing this book as well as his constant support, encouragement and patience with me throughout this process. I would like to thank my husband Jaym Wolfe for his excitement and encouragement in getting this material out there and for vision he sees with me in the amazing opportunities available to all through this work. I would also like to thank my son, Heritage, for his life and constant inspiration, for his hugs and laughter when I couldn't muster them myself, for his love of chocolate and his reminder of Spirit.

I thank my close friend and business partner, Terra Bundance, for her support—and for her stepping onto her path and into her truth so that I could see what that looks like. I thank her for seeing my book in its completion long ago, for her kindness, her spirit and her sisterhood and for her assistance in the editing process—with her insights; this book really began to make sense. I thank her beloved Michael Doss for his support in this process and believing in me and this message enough to help get it out there, for his help in the final editing of the book, which brought much of what I was wanting to say – to life! Thank you Michael, for hearing my heart and making me say it!!. I thank Terra for her love of chocolate and for her bravery in starting a raw chocolate business with me. You are the best! Terra not only are you my soul-sister best friend, but a truly inspirational woman who loves raw chocolate as much as I do and believes, as I do, that when you are passionate about something, you can change the world.

I want to thank Vickie Owens for her long-standing friendship and faith in me and every project I have ever undertaken; and for her willingness to support me in any way she can and her gentle, beautiful way of speaking her truth. I thank Rebecca Krishna Gayatri, one of my other soul-sisters on this journey of mine, for her enthusiasm, her blessings, and her presence with me when we get together, no matter how rarely this may be. She and I are on a very similar path, and I am so grateful for her seeing me through this process and helping me to remember where I came from and how short a journey this book process really was. And how awesome that is!!

I thank my mother for never failing to ask me how my book was coming along when we spoke on the phone, always encouraging me to finish it. Thank you to my sister Julie for telling me straight up that this was already a successful book, months before I had it finished, and for her constant encouragement, faithfulness, and her loving way. I thank my dad for being the wonderfully loving man he is, and for his excitement for me accomplishing something I really wanted to accomplish. Thank you to my sons grandparents, Kathy and Skip, for their love, and their proximity, which has made every aspect of this process—and life in general—so much easier and more pleasant than it would have been without them. (You're the best babysitters, ever!)

Thank you Master-mind group for the final push to get this out, and Jeff for helping with the final tweeks that made this publication happen!

I want to give special thanks to my teachers, who are many. Those who taught me the philosophy of yoga, the peace of meditation, the truth in myself, as well as those who taught me in an instant when I passed by them on the street and they offered me a genuine smile or a kind gesture. I thank those who have come into my life for however short or long a moment. I acknowledge that each soul has reflected a piece of myself for me, and that in leaving they never really left, but the their lessons and the our experiences continue to live in me and who I have become.

The awesome thing about change and growth and evolution is that we are all part of the process together—and from That we cannot separate ourselves. Thank you for the touch, the gaze, the word, the book, the laughter, the rhyme, the lesson, the trip, the forgiveness, and the love. Thank you for being you.

I want to thank every person in my life who has, in his or her own way, made this book possible. Thank you, Blessings, and may we all notice the Abundance that is around us and within us today! *Hari Om and Namaste!*

~Stasia Bliss, re-born into Bliss!

~All One